Classic
CAT STORIES

EDITED AND WITH
AN INTRODUCTION *by*
DEBORAH McHUGH

THE LYONS PRESS
GUILFORD, CONNECTICUT
AN IMPRINT OF THE GLOBE PEQUOT PRESS

The Lyons Press is an imprint of The Globe Pequot Press

Printed in the United States of America

10   9   8   7   6   5   4   3   2   1

Text Design by Claire Zoghb

ISBN 1-59228-255-5

Library of Congress Cataloging-in-Publication Data
is available on file.

To Jim, thank you for transportation services and to Oona and Oliver, who are not cats.

Contents

CONTENTS

CONTENTS

Introduction

[A UNIQUE MYSTIQUE]

A happy arrangement:
many people prefer *cats* to other people,
and many *cats* prefer people to other *cats.*
—*Mason Cooley*

This quotation struck me—a longtime cat-lover—as completely true. The natural question then becomes, why *do* cats prefer people? What prompted the first wild feline to forsake the safety of the shadows and venture toward the campfire of humankind? Unlike dogs, which were lured into domesticity by a combined need for the bounty and company of men, cats needed neither. Your average "tubby tabby" house cat of today could easily catch itself a mouse or a bird—cats' razor-sharp hunting and survival instincts have not been dulled over time like those of their canine counterparts. And what self-respecting cat has ever openly admitted needing affection or companionship? Yet there they are . . . those furry, finicky—and still surprisingly feral—creatures, who move in one day and take over our homes—and our hearts. It is just one of the many mysteries surrounding cats.

Humans have been beguiled by these mysteries since the time of the ancient Egyptians, when the cat goddess Bast, patron of pleasure and plenty, was revered, and pet cats were mummified so that they could eventually share the afterlife with their owners. Over time, Greeks and Romans, cardinals and kings, poets and playwrights, artists and actors, all appreciated the special allure of cats. Writers, especially, have always had an affinity for them and often used them for literary fodder. Sometimes it is the sly or ominous side of their feline natures that is the focus of these stories, but just as often it is other, more winning qualities—their beauty, self-containment, mercurial personalities, frenzied spirit of play. . . or that sudden need for a good cuddle—that compel authors to explore the unique mystique of cats.

This collection begins with two writers' exploration of this mystique. In his essay "The Cat," Andrew Barton Paterson explains a few facets of its many-sided character. H. H. Munro, better known as Saki, who is known best for another famous cat tale "Tobermory," also takes up the challenge of explaining what makes cats unique in the animal world in "The Achievement of the Cat." Both men conclude that it just may be the cat's innate dignity, strong will, and air of mystery.

The air of mystery that surrounds even the most tame house cat has led to their long association with the occult. A piece by folklorist Charles G. Leland, "How Diana Made the Stars and the Rain," comes from one of the most famous and controversial occult works, *Aradia; or the Gospel of the Witches,* and features the sister of Lucifer who turns herself into a cat—and finds a clever use for mice. While Leland brings us a mix of ancient Roman religion and Christianity (and a bit of fairy tale), Arthur Weigall, the famed Egyptologist who discovered the tomb of Tutankhamen, takes us to Luxor, Egypt, in a charming essay, "The Home Life of a Holy Cat." Like her namesake Bast, his pet Basta exuded a queenly air of mystery. Ancient Egypt—and its cat mummies—also held mysteries for Bram Stoker, creator of *Dracula.* In an excerpt from his lesser-known *The Jewel of the Seven Stars,* a live cat, Silvio, has an otherworldly reaction to its mummified kin.

Another otherworldly cat tale comes from the pen of one of the masters of horror and supernatural fiction, H. P. Lovecraft. "The Cats of Ulthar" is a menacing tale that demonstrates just why you should never kill a cat. Frederick Stuart Greene's sinister "The Cat of the Cane-Brake" also shows why you should never even threaten one, while occult writer Algernon Blackwood uses the mystery of feline qualities to frighten us in "An Empty Sleeve."

Master of mystery stories Sir Arthur Conan Doyle's "The Brazilian Cat" is not your average domesticated species (it appears to be a panther), although it *is* a house pet. But even the most socialized of the wild cats can prove deadly—and this one helps a penniless young fellow secure his rightful inheritance. Another story of an inheritance is "The White Cat" by W. W. Jacobs, where the welfare of one well-loved feline determines when one cat-hating man will inherit his uncle's property.

"Who Is to Blame?" by Anton Chekhov takes us away from the sinister and explores both human and feline nature—and how a cruel teacher can make either species lose even its most basic instincts. And in "The Philanthropist and the Happy Cat," we return to Saki for another look at human and feline nature, one that shows that we can learn a bit about contentment from our furry housemates.

The hero of A. S. Downs's "Plato: The Story of a Cat," is a perfect example of feline contentment. He revels in the amenities of his adopted home, especially his fine basket, and seems only concerned with his creature comforts. Cats, however, will always surprise their families—and Plato surprises his when he shows his tender side to raggedy stray. Yet, even the most indulged cats have a taste for adventure now and then. In a satirical piece from the April 9, 1905 edition of the *New York Times,* a reporter decides to dig out the full story of Bambino, cat-lover Mark Twain's lost pet.

A few cats have become the stuff of legend, and included here are a few of these extraordinary cats. Talking cats appear in "Ye Marvellous Legend of Tom Connor's Cat," a tale from nineteenth-century Irish novelist Samuel Lover, "Cat and King," a satirical fable from Ambrose Bierce, and of course, Charles Perrault's "Puss in Boots," which features one of the most famous literary cats of all time.

Even cats that cannot talk can prove to be wonderfully resourceful. In Charles G. D. Robinson's "The Cat Who Played Robinson Crusoe," an accidentally abandoned cat spends a long, hard winter alone on an island—and learns to fend for herself. Two others, W. L. Alden's "The Yellow Terror" and John Coleman Adams's "Midshipman, the Cat" adapt to life aboard ship, earning the admiration of their fellow sailors.

The final stories in this collection feature cats who do nothing special—other than excelling at just being cats. "Peter: A Cat o' One Tail" is the chronicle of one cat that illustrates some of the delights in sharing our lives with a feline companion, while the sixteenth-century French essayist Montaigne offers a thought about just who amuses the other more: human or cat? And finally, Calvin, the much-loved cat of writer Charles Dudley Warner, receives a heartwarming homage in "Calvin: A Study of a Character." As did Warner, inevitably, most of us have to face saying goodbye to our best friends, but we never forget them. No matter how many cats we have, each one of them always has its own unique mystique.

The Cat

[ANDREW BARTON PATERSON]

Most people think that the cat is an unintelligent animal, fond of ease, and caring little for anything but mice and milk. But a cat has really more character than most human beings, and gets a great deal more satisfaction out of life. Of all the animal kingdom, the cat has the most many-sided character.

He—or she—is an athlete, a musician, an acrobat, a Lothario, a grim fighter, a sport of the first water. All day long the cat loafs about the house, takes things easy, sleeps by the fire, and allows himself to be pestered by the attentions of our womenfolk and annoyed by our children. To pass the time away he sometimes watches a mouse-hole for an hour or two—just to keep himself from dying of ennui; and people get the idea that this sort of thing is all that life holds for the cat. But watch him as the shades of evening fall, and you see the cat as he really is.

When the family sits down to tea, the cat usually puts in an appearance to get his share, and purrs noisily, and rubs himself against the legs of the family; and all the time he is thinking of a fight or a love-affair that is coming off that evening. If there is a guest at table the cat is particularly civil to him, because the guest is likely to have the best of what is going. Sometimes, instead of recognizing this civility with something to eat, the guest stoops down and strokes the cat, and says, "Poor pussy! poor pussy!"

The cat soon tires of that; he puts up his claw and quietly but firmly rakes the guest in the leg.

"Ow!" says the guest, "the cat stuck his claws into me!" The delighted family remarks, "Isn't it sweet of him? Isn't he intelligent? *He wants you to give him something to eat.*"

The guest dares not do what he would like to do—kick the cat through the window—so, with tears of rage and pain in his eyes, he affects to be very much amused, and sorts out a bit of fish from his plate and hands it down. The cat gingerly receives it, with a look in his eyes that says: "Another time, my friend, you won't be so dull of comprehension," and purrs maliciously as he retires to a safe distance from the guest's boot before eating it. A cat isn't a fool—not by a long way.

When the family has finished tea, and gathers round the fire to enjoy the hours of indigestion, the cat slouches casually out of the room and disappears. Life, true life, now begins for him.

He saunters down his own backyard, springs to the top of the fence with one easy bound, drops lightly down on the other side, trots across the right-of-way to a vacant allotment, and skips to the roof of an empty shed. As he goes, he throws off the effeminacy of civilization; his gait becomes lithe and panther-like; he looks quickly and keenly from side to side, and moves noiselessly, for he has so many enemies—dogs, cabmen with whips, and small boys with stones.

Arrived on the top of the shed, the cat arches his back, rakes his claws once or twice through the soft bark of the old roof, wheels round and stretches himself a few times; just to see that every muscle is in full working order; then, dropping his head nearly to his paws, he sends across a league of backyards his call to his kindred—a call to love, or war, or sport.

Before long they come, gliding, graceful shadows, approaching circuitously, and halting occasionally to reconnoiter—tortoiseshell, tabby, and black, all domestic cats, but all transformed for the nonce into their natural state. No longer are they the hypocritical, meek creatures who an hour ago were cadging for fish and milk. They are now ruffling, swaggering blades with a Gascon sense of dignity. Their fights are grim and determined, and a cat will be clawed to ribbons before he will yield.

Even young lady cats have this inestimable superiority over human beings, that they can work off jealousy, hatred, and malice in a sprawling, yelling combat on a flat roof. All cats fight, and all keep themselves more or less in training while they are young. Your cat may be the acknowledged lightweight champion of his district—a Griffo of the feline ring!

Just think how much more he gets out of his life than you do out of yours—what a hurricane of fighting and lovemaking his life is—and blush for yourself. You have had one little love affair, and never had a good, all-out fight in your life!

And the sport they have, too! As they get older and retire from the ring they go in for sport more systematically; the suburban backyards, that are to us but dullness indescribable, are to them hunting-grounds and trysting-places where they may have more gallant adventure than ever had King Arthur's knights or Robin Hood's merry men.

Grimalkin decides to kill a canary in a neighboring verandah. Consider the fascination of it—the stealthy reconnaissance from the top of the fence; the care to avoid waking the house-dog, the noiseless approach and the hurried dash, and the fierce clawing at the fluttering bird till its mangled body is dragged through the bars of the cage; the exultant retreat with the spoil; the growling over the feast that follows. Not the least entertaining part of it is the demure satisfaction of arriving home in time for breakfast and hearing the house-mistress say: "Tom must be sick; he seems to have no appetite."

It is always leveled as a reproach against cats that they are more fond of their home than of the people in it. Naturally, the cat doesn't like to leave his country, the land where all his friends are, and where he knows every landmark. Exiled in a strange land, he would have to learn a new geography, to exploit another tribe of dogs, to fight and make love to an entirely new nation of cats. Life isn't long enough for that sort of thing.

So, when the family moves, the cat, if allowed, will stay at the old house and attach himself to the new tenants. He will give them the privilege of boarding him while he enjoys life in his own way. He is not going to sacrifice his whole career for the doubtful reward which fidelity to his old master or mistress might bring.

The Achievement of the Cat

[**SAKI**]

In the political history of nations it is no uncommon experience to find States and peoples which but a short time since were in bitter conflict and animosity with each other, settled down comfortably on terms of mutual goodwill and even alliance. The natural history of the social developments of species affords a similar instance in the coming-together of two once warring elements, now represented by civilized man and the domestic cat. The fiercely waged struggle which went on between humans and felines in those far-off days when sabre-toothed tiger and cave lion contended with primeval man, has long ago been decided in favor of the most fitly equipped combatant—the Thing with a Thumb—and the descendants of the dispossessed family are relegated today, for the most part, to the waste lands of jungle and veld, where an existence of self-effacement is the only alternative to extermination. But the *felis catus,* or whatever species was the ancestor of the modern domestic cat (a vexed question at present), by a master-stroke of adaptation avoided the ruin of its race, and "captured" a place in the very keystone of the conqueror's organization. For not as a bondservant or dependent has this proudest of mammals entered the human fraternity; not as a slave like the beasts of burden, or a humble camp-follower like the dog. The cat is domestic only as far as suits its own ends; it will not be kenneled or harnessed nor suffer any dictation as to its goings out or comings in. Long contact with the human race has developed in it the art of diplomacy, and no Roman Cardinal of mediæval days knew better how to ingratiate himself with his surroundings than a cat with a saucer of cream on its mental horizon. But the social smoothness, the purring innocence, the softness of the velvet paw may be laid aside at a moment's notice, and the sinuous feline may disappear, in deliberate aloofness, to a world of roofs and chimney-stacks, where the human element is distanced and disregarded. Or the innate savage spirit that helped its survival in the bygone days of tooth and claw may be summoned forth from beneath the sleek exterior, and the torture-instinct (common alone to human and feline) may find free play in the death-throes of some luckless bird or rodent. It is, indeed, no small triumph to have combined the untrammeled liberty of primeval savagery with the luxury which only a highly developed civilization can command; to be lapped in the soft stuffs that commerce has gathered from the far ends of the world, to bask in the warmth that labor and industry have dragged from the bowels of the earth; to banquet on the dainties that wealth has bespoken for its table, and withal to be a free son of nature, a mighty hunter, a spiller of life-blood. This is the victory of the cat. But besides the credit of success the cat has other qualities which compel recognition. The animal which the Egyptians worshipped as divine, which the Romans venerated as a symbol of liberty, which Europeans in the ignorant Middle Ages anathematized as an agent of demonology, has displayed to all ages two closely blended characteristics—courage and self-respect. No matter how unfavorable the circumstances, both qualities are always to the fore. Confront a child, a puppy, and a kitten with a sudden danger; the child will turn instinctively for assistance, the puppy will grovel in abject submission to the impending visitation, the kitten will brace its tiny body for a frantic resistance. And disassociate the luxury-loving cat from the atmosphere of social comfort in which it usually contrives to move, and observe it critically under the adverse conditions of civilization—that civilization which can impel a man to the degradation of clothing himself in tawdry ribald garments and capering mountebank dances in the streets for the earning of the few coins that keep him on the respectable, or non-criminal, side of society. The cat of the slums and alleys, starved, outcast, harried, still keeps amid the prowlings of its adversity the bold, free, panther-tread with which it paced of yore the temple courts of Thebes, still displays the self-reliant watchfulness which man has never taught it to lay aside. And when its shifts and clever managings have not sufficed to stave off inexorable fate, when its enemies have proved too strong or too many for its defensive powers, it dies fighting to the last, quivering with the choking rage or mastered resistance, and voicing in its death-yell that agony of bitter remonstrance which human animals, too, have flung at the powers that may be; the last protest against a destiny that might have made them happy—and has not.

How Diana Made the Stars and the Rain

[CHARLES G. LELAND]

Diana was the first created before all creation; in her were all things; out of herself, the first darkness, she divided herself; into darkness and light she was divided. Lucifer, her brother and son, herself and her other half, was the light.

And when Diana saw that the light was so beautiful, the light which was her other half, her brother Lucifer, she yearned for it with exceeding great desire. Wishing to receive the light again into her darkness, to swallow it up in rapture, in delight, she trembled with desire. This desire was the Dawn.

But Lucifer, the light, fled from her, and would not yield to her wishes; he was the light which flies into the most distant parts of heaven, the mouse which flies before the cat.

Then Diana went to the fathers of the Beginning, to the mothers, the spirits who were before the first spirit, and lamented unto them that she could not prevail with Lucifer. And they praised her for her courage, they told her that to rise she must fall; to become the chief of goddesses she must become a mortal.

And in the ages, in the course of time, when the world was made, Diana went on earth, as did Lucifer, who had fallen, and Diana taught magic and sorcery, whence came witches and fairies and goblins—all that is like man, yet not mortal.

And it came thus that Diana took the form of a cat. Her brother had a cat whom he loved beyond all creatures, and it slept every night on his bed, a cat beautiful beyond all other creatures, a fairy: he did not know it.

Diana prevailed with the cat to change forms with her, so she lay with her brother, and in the darkness assumed her own form, and so by Lucifer became the mother of Aradia. But when in the morning he found that he lay by his sister, and that light had been conquered by darkness, Lucifer was extremely angry; but Diana sang to him a spell, a song of power, and he was silent, the song of the night which soothes to sleep; he could say nothing. So Diana with her wiles of witchcraft so charmed him that he yielded to her love. This was the first fascination, she hummed the song, it was as the buzzing of bees (or a top spinning round), a spinning-wheel spinning life. She spun the lives of all men; all things were spun from the wheel of Diana. Lucifer turned the wheel.

Diana was not known to the witches and spirits, the fairies and elves who dwell in desert place, the goblins, as their mother; she hid herself in humility and was a mortal, but by her will she rose again above all. She had such passion for witchcraft, and became so powerful therein, that her greatness could not be hidden.

And thus it came to pass one night, at the meeting of all the sorceresses and fairies, she declared that she would darken the heavens and turn all the stars into mice.

All those who were present said—

"If thou canst do such a strange thing, having risen to such power, thou shalt be our queen."

Diana went into the street; she took the bladder of an ox and a piece of witch-money, which has an edge like a knife—with such money witches cut the earth from men's foot-tracks—and she cut the earth, and with it and many mice she filled the bladder, and blew into the bladder till it burst.

And there came a great marvel, for the earth which was in the bladder became the round heaven above, and for three days there was a great rain; the mice became stars or rain. And having made the heaven and the stars and the rain, Diana became Queen of the Witches; she was the cat who ruled the star-mice, the heaven and the rain.

The Home Life of a Holy Cat

[ARTHUR WEIGALL]

One summer during a heat wave, when the temperature in the shade of my veranda in Luxor was 125 degrees Fahrenheit, I went down to cooler Lower Egypt to pay a visit to an English friend of mine stationed at Zagazig, the native city which stands beside the ruins of ancient Bubastis.

He was about to leave Egypt and asked me whether I would like to have his cat, a dignified, mystical-minded, long-legged, small-headed, green-eyed female, whose orange-yellow hair, marked with grayish black stripes in tabby pattern, was so short that she gave the impression of being naked—an impression, however, which did not in any way detract from her air of virginal chastity.

Her name was Basta, and though recent ancestors had lived wild amongst the ruins, she was so obviously a descendant of holy cats of ancient times, who were incarnations of the goddess Basta, that I thought it only right to accept the offer and take her to Luxor to live with me. To be the expert in charge of Egyptian antiquities and not have an ancient Egyptian cat to give an air of mystery to my headquarters had, indeed, always seemed to me to be somewhat wanting in showmanship on my part.

Thus it came about that, on my departure, I drove off to the railroad station with the usually dignified Basta bumping around and uttering unearthly howls inside a cardboard hatbox, in the side of which I had cut a small round hole for ventilation. The people in the streets and on the station platform seemed to be under the impression that the noises were digestive and that I was in dire need of a doctor; and it was a great relief to my embarrassment when the hot and panting train steamed in Zagazig.

Fortunately, I found myself alone in the compartment, and the hatbox at my side had begun to cause me less anxiety, when suddenly Basta was seized with a sort of religious frenzy. The box rocked about, and presently out through the airhole came a long, snakelike paw which pushed itself outward with such frantic force that the sides of the hole gave way, and out burst the entire sandy, sacred head.

She then began to choke, for the cardboard was pressing tightly around her neck; and to save her from strangulation I was obliged to tear the aperture open, whereupon she wriggled out, leaped in divine frenzy up the side of the carriage and prostrated herself on the network of the baggage-rack, where her hysteria caused her to lose all control of her internal arrangements if and I say modestly that she was overcome with nausea, I shall be telling but a part of the dreadful tale.

The rest of the journey was like a bad dream; but at the Cairo terminus, where I had to change into the night express for Luxor, I got the help of a native policeman who secured a large laundry basket from the sleeping-car department. And after a prolonged struggle, during which the train was shunted into a distant siding, we imprisoned the struggling Basta again.

The perspiring policeman and I then carried the basket at a run along the tracks back to the station in the sweltering heat of the late afternoon, and I just managed to catch my train; but during the second part of my journey Basta traveled in the baggage-van whence, in the hot and silent night, whenever we were at a standstill, her appalling incantations came drifting to my ears.

I opened the basket in an unfurnished spare room in my house, and like a flash Basta was up the bare wall and onto the curtain pole above the window. There she remained all day, in a sort of hypnotic trance; but at sunset the saucer of milk and plate of fish which I had provided for her at last enticed her down, and in the end she reconciled herself to her new surroundings and indicated by her behavior that she was willing to accept my house as her earthly temple.

With Pedro, my pariah dog, there was not the slightest trouble; he had no strong feelings about cats, and she on her part graciously deigned to acknowledge his status—as, I believe, is generally the case in native households. She sometimes condescended to visit my horse and donkey in their stalls; and for Laura, my camel, she quickly developed a real regard, often sleeping for hours in her stable.

I was not worried as to how she would treat the chickens and pigeons, because her former owner in Zagazig had insisted upon her respecting his hen coop and pigeon cote; but I was a little anxious about the ducks, for she had not previously known any, and in ancient times her ancestors used to be trained to hunt wild geese and ducks and were fed with *pâté de foie gras,* or whatever it was called then, on holy days and anniversaries.

In a corner of the garden I had made a miniature duck pond which was sunk rather deeply in the ground and down to which I had cut a narrow, steeply sloping passage, or gangway. During the day, after the ducks had been up and down this slope several times, the surface used to become wet and slippery, and the ducks, having waddled down the first few inches, were forced to toboggan down the rest of it on their tails, with their two feet sticking out in front of them and their heads well up.

Basta was always fascinated by this slide and by the splash at the bottom and used to sit and watch it for hours, which made me think at first that she would one day spring at one of them; but she never did. Field mice, and water rats down by the Nile, were her only prey; and in connection with the former I may mention a curious occurrence.

One hot night I was sitting smoking my pipe on the veranda when my attention was attracted by two mice which had crept into the patch of brilliant moonlight before my feet and were boldly nibbling some crumbs left over from a cracker thrown to Pedro earlier in the evening. I watched them silently for a while and did not notice that Basta had seen them and was preparing to spring, nor did I observe a large white owl sitting aloft amongst the overhanging roses and also preparing to pounce.

Suddenly, and precisely at the same moment, the owl shot down on the mice from above and Basta leaped at them from beside me. There was a scuffle; fur and feathers flew; I fell out of my chair; and then the owl made off screeching in one direction and the cat dashed away on the other; while the mice, practically clinging to each other, remained for a moment or two too terrified to move.

During the early days of her residence in Luxor, Basta often used to go down to the edge of the Nile to fish with her paw; but she never caught anything, and in the end she got a fright and gave it up. I was sitting by the river watching her tying to catch one of the little shoal of small fish which were sunning themselves in the shallow water when there came swimming into view a twelve- or fourteen-inch fish which I recognized (by its whiskers and the absence of a dorsal fin) as the electric catfish, pretty common in the Nile—a strange creature able to give you an electric shock like hitting your funny bone.

These fish obtain their food in a curious way: they hang around any shoal of small fry engaged in feeding, and then glide quietly into their midst and throw out this electric shock, whereupon the little fellows are all sick to their stomachs, and the big fellow gets their disgorged dinners.

I was just waiting to see this happen with my own eyes—for it had always seemed a bit farfetched—when Basta made a dart at the intruder with her paw and got a shock. She uttered a yowl as though somebody had trodden on her and leaped high in the air;

and never again did she put a foot near the water. She was content after that with our daily offering of a fish brought from the market and fried for her like a burnt sacrifice.

Basta had a most unearthly voice, and when she was feeling emotional would let out a wail which at first was like the crying of a phantom baby and then became the tuneless song of a lunatic, and finally developed into the blood-curdling howl of a soul in torment. And when she spat, the percussion was like that of a spring-gun.

There were some wild cats or, rather, domestic cats who, like Basta's own forebears, had taken to a wild life, living in a grove of trees beside the river just beyond my garden wall; and it was generally the proximity of one of these which started her off; but sometimes the outburst was caused by her own unfathomable thoughts as she went her mysterious ways in the darkness of the night.

I think she must have been clairvoyant, for she often seemed to be seeing things not visible to me. Sometimes, perhaps when she was cleaning fish or mouse from her face, she would pause with one foot off the ground and stare in front of her, and then back away with bristling hair or go forward with friendly mewing noises; and sometimes she would leap off a chair or sofa, her tail lashing and her green eyes dilated. But it may have been worms.

Once I saw her standing absolutely rigid and tense on the lawn, staring at the rising moon; and then all of a sudden she did a sort of dance such as cats do sometimes when they are playing with other cats. But there was no other cat and, anyway, Basta never played; she never forgot that she was a holy cat.

Her chaste hauteur was so great that she would not move out of the way when people were walking about, and many a time her demoniacal shriek and perhaps a crash of breaking glass informed the household that somebody had tripped over her. It was astonishing, however, how quickly she recovered her dignity and how well she maintained the pretence that whatever happened to her was at her own celestial wish and was not our doing.

If I called her she would pretend not to hear, but would come a few moments later when it could appear that she had thought of doing so first; and if I lifted her off a chair she would jump back up on it and then descend with dignity as though of her own free will. But in this, of course, she was more like a woman than a divinity.

The Egyptian cat is a domesticated species of the African wildcat, and no doubt its strange behavior and its weird voice were the cause of it being regarded as sacred in ancient times; but, although the old gods and their worship have been forgotten these many centuries, the traditional sanctity of the race has survived.

Modern Egyptians think it unlucky to hurt a cat and, in the native quarters of Cairo and other cities, hundreds of cats are daily fed at the expense of benevolent citizens. They say that they do this because cats are so useful to mankind in killing off mice and other pests; but actually it is an unrecognized survival of the old beliefs.

In the days of the Pharaohs, when a cat died the men of the household shaved off their eyebrows and sat around wailing and rocking themselves to and fro in simulated anguish. The body was embalmed and buried with solemn rites in the local cats' cemetery, or was sent down to Bubastis to rest in the shadow of the temple of their patron goddess. I myself have dug up hundreds of mummified cats; and once, when I had a couple dozen of the best specimens standing on my veranda waiting to be dispatched to the Cairo Museum, Basta was most excited about it, and walked around sniffing at them all day. They certainly smelled awful.

On my lawn there was a square slab of stone which had once been the top of an altar dedicated to the sun god, but was now used as a sort of low garden table; and sometimes when she had caught a mouse she used to deposit the chewed corpse upon this slab—nobody could think why, unless, as I always told people, she was really making an offering to the sun. It was most mysterious of her; but it led once to a very unfortunate episode.

A famous French antiquarian, who was paying a polite call, was sitting with me beside this sacred stone, drinking afternoon tea and eating fresh dates, when Basta appeared on the scene with a small dead mouse in her mouth, which in her usual way she deposited upon the slab—only on this occasion she laid it on my guest's plate, which was standing on the slab.

We were talking at the moment and did not see her do this and, anyhow, the Frenchman was as blind as a bat; and, of course, as luck would have it, he immediately picked up the wet, mole-colored mouse instead of a ripe brown date, and the thing has almost gone into his mouth before he saw what it was and, with a yell, flung it into the air.

It fell into his upturned sun helmet which was lying on the grass beside him; but he did not see where it had gone and, jumping angrily to his feet in the momentary belief that I had played a schoolboy joke on him, he snatched up his helmet and was in the act of putting it on his head when the mouse tumbled out onto the front of his shirt and slipped down inside his buttoned jacket.

At this he went more or less mad, danced about, shook himself, and finally trod on Basta, who completed his frenzy by uttering a fiendish howl and digging her claws into his leg. The dead mouse, I am glad to say, fell onto the grass during the dance without it passing through his roomy trousers, as I had feared it might; and Basta, recovering her dignity, picked it up and walked off with it.

It is a remarkable fact that, during the five or six years she spent with me, she showed no desire to be anything but a spinster all her life, and when I arranged a marriage for her she displayed such dignified but violent antipathy towards the bridegroom that the match was a failure. In the end, however, she fell in love with one of the wild cats who lived among the trees beyond my wall, and nothing could prevent her from going off to visit him from time to time, generally at dead of night.

He did not care a hoot about her sanctity, and she was feminine enough to enjoy the novelty of being roughly treated. I never actually saw him, for he did not venture into the garden, but I used to hear him knocking her about the outside garden gates; and when she came home, scratched and bitten and muttering something about holy cats, it was plain that she was desperately happy. She licked her wounds, indeed, with deep voluptuous satisfaction.

A dreadful change came over her. She lost her precious dignity and was restless and inclined to be savage; her digestion played embarrassing tricks on her; and once she mortally offended Laura by claw-ing her nose. There was a new glint in her green eyes as she watched the ducks sliding into the pond; the pigeons interested her for the first time; and for the first time, too, she *ate* the mice she had caught.

Then she began to disappear for a whole day or night at a time, and once when I went in search of her amongst the trees outside and found her sharp-ening her claws on a branch above my head, she put her ears back and hissed at me until I could see halfway down her pink throat. I tried by every method to keep her at home when she came back, but it was all in vain, and at last she left me forever.

Weeks afterwards I caught sight of her once again amongst the trees, and it was evident that she was soon to become a mother. She gave me a friendly mew this time; but she would not let me touch her; and presently she slipped away into the under-growth. I never knew what became of her.

The Watchers

BRAM STOKER

My Dear Daughter:

I want you to take this letter as an instruction—absolute and imperative, and admitting of no deviation whatever—in case anything untoward or unexpected by you or by others should happen to me. If I should be suddenly and mysteriously stricken down—either by sickness, accident or attack—you must follow these directions implicitly. If I am not already in my bedroom when you are made cognizant of my state, I am to be brought there as quickly as possible. Even should I be dead, my body is to be brought there. Thenceforth, until I am either conscious and able to give instructions on my own account, or buried, I am never to be left alone—not for a single instant. From nightfall to sunrise at least two persons must remain in the room. It will be well that a trained nurse be in the room from time to time, and will note any symptoms, either permanent or changing, which may strike her. My solicitors, Marvin & Jewkes, of 27B Lincoln's Inn, have full instructions in case of my death; and Mr. Marvin has himself undertaken to see personally my wishes carried out. I should advise you, my dear Daughter, seeing that you have no relative to apply to, to get some friend whom you can trust to either remain within the house where instant communication can be made, or to come nightly to aid in the watching, or to be within call. Such friend may be either male or female; but, whichever it may be, there should be added one other watcher or attendant at hand of the opposite sex. Understand, that it is of the very essence of my wish that there should be, awake and exercising themselves to my purposes, both masculine and feminine intelligences. Once more, my dear Margaret, let me impress on you the need for observation and just reasoning to conclusions, howsoever strange. If I am taken ill or injured, this will be no ordinary occasion; and I wish to warn you, so that your guarding may be complete.

Nothing in my room—I speak of the curios—must be removed or displaced in any way, or for any cause whatever. I have a special reason and a special purpose in the placing of each; so that any moving of them would thwart my plans.

Should you want money or counsel in anything, Mr. Marvin will carry out your wishes; to the which he has my full instructions.

Abel Trelawny

...THAT NIGHT WE WERE NOT YET REGULARLY organized for watching, so that the early part of the evening showed an unevenly balanced guard. Nurse Kennedy, who had been on duty all day, was lying down, as she had arranged to come on again by twelve o'clock. Doctor Winchester, who was dining in the house, remained in the room until dinner was announced; and went back at once when it was over. During dinner Mrs. Grant remained in the room, and with her Sergeant Daw, who wished to complete a minute examination which he had undertaken of everything in the room and near it. At nine o'clock Miss Trelawny and I went in to relieve the Doctor. She had lain down for a few hours in the afternoon so as to be refreshed for her work at night. She told me that she had determined that for this night at least she would sit up and watch. I did not try to dissuade her, for I knew that her mind was made up. Then and there I made up my mind that I would watch with her—unless, of course, I should see that she really did not wish it. I said nothing of my intentions for the present. We came in on tiptoe, so silently that the Doctor, who was bending over the bed, did not hear us, and seemed a little startled when suddenly looking up he saw our eyes upon him. I felt that the mystery of the whole thing was getting on his nerves, as it had already got on the nerves of some others of us. He was, I fancied, a little annoyed with himself for having been so startled, and at once began to talk in a hurried manner as though to get over our idea of his embarrassment:

"I am really and absolutely at my wits' end to find any fit cause for this stupor. I have made again as accurate an examination as I know how, and I am satisfied that there is no injury to the brain, that is, no external injury. Indeed, all his vital organs seem unimpaired. I have given him, as you know, food several times and it has manifestly done him good. His breathing is strong and regular, and his pulse is slower and stronger than it was this morning. I cannot find evidence of any known drug, and his unconsciousness does not resemble any of the many cases of hypnotic sleep which I saw in the Charcot Hospital in Paris. And as to these wounds"—he laid his finger gently on the bandaged wrist which lay outside the coverlet as he spoke—"I do not know what to make of them. They might have been made by a carding-machine; but that supposition is untenable. It is within the bounds of possibility that they might have been made by a wild animal if it had taken care to sharpen its claws. That too is, I take it, impossible. By the way, have you any strange pets here in the house; anything of an exceptional kind, such as a tiger-cat or anything out of the common?" Miss Trelawny smiled a sad smile which made my heart ache, as she made answer:

"Oh no! Father does not like animals about the house, unless they are dead and mummied." This was said with a touch of bitterness—or jealousy, I could hardly tell which. "Even my poor kitten was only allowed in the house on sufferance; and though he is the dearest and best-conducted cat in the world, he is now on a sort of parole, and is not allowed into this room."

As she was speaking a faint rattling of the door handle was heard. Instantly Miss Trelawny's face brightened. She sprang up and went over to the door, saying as she went:

"There he is! That is my Silvio. He stands on his hind legs and rattles the door handle when he wants to come into a room." She opened the door, speaking to the cat as though he were a baby: "Did him want his movver? Come then; but he must stay with her!" She lifted the cat, and came back with him in her arms. He was certainly a magnificent animal. A chinchilla grey Persian with long silky hair; a really lordly animal with a haughty bearing despite his gentleness; and with great paws which spread out as he placed them on the ground. Whilst she was fondling him, he suddenly gave a wriggle like an eel and slipped out of her arms. He ran across the room and stood opposite a low table on which stood the mummy of an animal, and began to mew and snarl. Miss Trelawny was after him in an instant and lifted him in her arms, kicking and struggling and wriggling to get away; but not biting or scratching, for evidently he loved his beautiful mistress. He ceased to make a noise the moment he was in her arms; in a whisper she admonished him:

"O you naughty Silvio! You have broken your parole that mother gave for you. Now, say goodnight to the gentlemen, and come away to mother's room!" As she was speaking she held out the cat's paw to me to shake. As I did so I could not but admire its size and beauty. "Why," said I, "his paw seems like a little boxing-glove full of claws." She smiled:

"So it ought to. Don't you notice that my Silvio has seven toes, see!" she opened the paw; and surely enough there were seven separate claws, each of them sheathed in a delicate, fine, shell-like case. As I gently stroked the foot the claws emerged and one of them accidentally—there was no anger now and the cat was purring—stuck into my hand. Instinctively I said as I drew back:

"Why, his claws are like razors!"

Doctor Winchester had come close to us and was bending over looking at the cat's claws; as I spoke he said in a quick, sharp way:

"Eh!" I could hear the quick intake of his breath. Whilst I was stroking the now quiescent cat, the Doctor went to the table and tore off a piece of blotting-paper from the writing-pad and came back. He laid the paper on his palm and, with a simple "pardon me!" to Miss Trelawny, placed the cat's paw on it and pressed it down with his other hand. The haughty cat seemed to resent somewhat the familiarity, and tried to draw its foot away. This was plainly what the Doctor wanted, for in the act the cat opened the sheaths of its claws and made several reefs in the soft paper. Then Miss Trelawny took her pet away. She returned in a couple of minutes; as she came in she said:

"It is most odd about that mummy! When Silvio came into the room first—indeed I took him in as a kitten to show to Father—he went on just the same way. He jumped up on the table, and tried to scratch and bite the mummy. That was what made Father so angry, and brought the decree of banishment on poor Silvio. Only his parole, given through me, kept him in the house."

Whilst she had been gone, Doctor Winchester had taken the bandage from her father's wrist. The wound was now quite clear, as the separate cuts showed out in fierce red lines. The Doctor folded the blotting-paper across the line of punctures made by the cat's claws, and held it down close to the wound. As he did so, he looked up triumphantly and beckoned us over to him.

The cuts in the paper corresponded with the wounds in the wrist! No explanation was needed, as he said:

"It would have been better if master Silvio had not broken his parole!"

We were all silent for a little while. Suddenly Miss Trelawny said:

"But Silvio was not in here last night!"

"Are you sure? Could you prove that if necessary?" She hesitated before replying:

"I am certain of it; but I fear it would be difficult to prove. Silvio sleeps in a basket in my room. I certainly put him to bed last night; I remember distinctly laying his little blanket over him, and tucking him in. This morning I took him out of the basket myself. I certainly never noticed him in here; though, of course, that would not mean much, for I was too concerned about poor father, and too much occupied with him, to notice even Silvio."

The Doctor shook his head as he said with a certain sadness:

"Well, at any rate it is no use trying to prove anything now. Any cat in the world would have cleaned blood-marks—did any exist—from his paws in a hundredth part of the time that has elapsed."

Again we were all silent; and again the silence was broken by Miss Trelawny:

"But now that I think of it, it could not have been poor Silvio that injured Father. My door was shut when I first heard the sound; and Father's was shut when I listened at it. When I went in, the injury had been done; so that it must have been before Silvio could possibly have got in." This reasoning commended itself, especially to me as a barrister, for it was proof to satisfy a jury. It gave me a distinct pleasure to have Silvio acquitted of the crime—possibly because he was Miss Trelawny's cat and was loved by her. Happy cat! Silvio's mistress was manifestly pleased as I said:

"Verdict, 'not guilty!'" Doctor Winchester after a pause observed:

"My apologies to master Silvio on this occasion; but I am still puzzled to know why he is so keen against that mummy. Is he the same toward the other mummies in the house? There are, I suppose, a lot of them. I saw three in the hall as I came in."

"There are lots of them," she answered. "I sometimes don't know whether I am in a private house or the British Museum. But Silvio never concerns himself about any of them except that particular one. I suppose it must be because it is of an animal, not a man or a woman."

"Perhaps it is of a cat!" said the Doctor as he started up and went across the room to look at the mummy more closely. "Yes," he went on, "it is the mummy of a cat; and a very fine one, too. If it hadn't been a special favorite of some very special person it would never have received so much honor. See! A painted case and obsidian eyes—just like a human mummy. It is an extraordinary thing, that knowledge of kind to kind. Here is a dead cat—that is all; it is perhaps four or five thousand years old—and another cat of another breed, in what is practically another world, is ready to fly at it, just as it would if it were not dead. I should like to experiment a bit about that cat if you don't mind, Miss Trelawny." She hesitated before replying:

"Of course, do anything you may think necessary or wise; but I hope it will not be anything to hurt or worry my poor Silvio." The Doctor smiled as he answered:

"Oh, Silvio would be all right: it is the other one that my sympathies would be reserved for."

"How do you mean?"

"Master Silvio will do the attacking; the other one will do the suffering."

"Suffering?" There was a note of pain in her voice. The Doctor smiled more broadly:

"Oh, please make your mind easy as to that. The other won't suffer as we understand it; except perhaps in his structure and outfit."

"What on earth do you mean?"

"Simply this, my dear young lady, that the antagonist will be a mummy cat like this one. There are, I take it, plenty of them to be had in Museum Street. I shall get one and place it here instead of that one—you won't think that a temporary exchange will violate your Father's instructions, I hope. We shall then find out, to begin with, whether Silvio objects to all mummy cats, or only to this one in particular."

"I don't know," she said doubtfully. "Father's instructions seem very uncompromising." Then after a pause she went on: "But of course under the circumstances anything that is to be ultimately for his good must be done. I suppose there can't be anything very particular about the mummy of a cat."

Doctor Winchester said nothing. He sat rigid, with so grave a look on his face that his extra gravity passed on to me; and in its enlightening perturbation I began to realize more than I had yet done the strangeness of the case in which I was now so deeply concerned. When once this thought had begun there was no end to it. Indeed it grew, and blossomed, and reproduced itself in a thousand different ways. The room and all in it gave grounds for strange thoughts. There were so many ancient relics that unconsciously one was taken back to strange lands and strange times. There were so many mummies or mummy objects, round which there seemed to cling for ever the penetrating odors of bitumen, and spices and gums—"Nard and Circassia's balmy smells"— that one was unable to forget the past. Of course, there was but little light in the room, and that carefully shaded; so that there was no glare anywhere. None of that direct light which can manifest itself as a power or an entity, and so make for companionship. The room was a large one, and lofty in proportion to its size. In its vastness was place for a multitude of things not often found in a bedchamber. In far corners of the room were shadows of uncanny shape. More than once as I thought, the multitudinous presence of the dead and the past took such hold on me that I caught myself looking round fearfully as though some strange personality or influence was present. Even the manifest presence of Doctor Winchester and Miss Trelawny could not altogether comfort or satisfy me at such moments. It was with a distinct sense of relief that I saw a new personality in the room in the shape of Nurse Kennedy. There was no doubt that that business-like, self-reliant, capable young woman added an element of security to such wild imaginings as my own. She had a quality of common sense that seemed to pervade everything around her, as though it were some kind of emanation. Up to that moment I had been building fancies around the sick man; so that finally all about him, including myself, had become involved in them, or enmeshed, or saturated, or . . . But now that she had come, he relapsed into his proper perspective as a patient; the room was a sickroom, and the shadows lost their fearsome quality. The only thing which it could not altogether abrogate was the strange Egyptian smell. You may put a mummy in a glass case and hermetically seal it so that no corroding air can get within; but all the same it will exhale its odor. One might think that four or five thousand years would exhaust the olfactory qualities of anything; but experience teaches us that these smells remain, and that their secrets are unknown to us. Today they are as much mysteries as they were when the embalmers put the body in the bath of natron . . .

All at once I sat up. I had become lost in an absorbing reverie. The Egyptian smell had seemed to get on my nerves—on my memory—on my very will.

At that moment I had a thought which was like an inspiration. If I was influenced in such a manner by the smell, might it not be that the sick man, who lived half his life or more in the atmosphere, had gradually and by slow but sure process taken into his system something which had permeated him to such degree that it had a new power derived from quantity—or strength—or . . .

I was becoming lost again in a reverie. This would not do. I must take such precaution that I could remain awake, or free from such entrancing thought. I had had but half a night's sleep last night; and this night I must remain awake. Without stating my intention, for I feared that I might add to the trouble and uneasiness of Miss Trelawny, I went downstairs and out of the house. I soon found a chemist's shop, and came away with a respirator. When I got back, it was ten o'clock; the Doctor was going for the night. The Nurse came with him to the door of the sick-room, taking her last instructions. Miss Trelawny sat still beside the bed. Sergeant Daw, who had entered as the Doctor went out, was some little distance off.

When Nurse Kennedy joined us, we arranged that she should sit up till two o'clock, when Miss Trelawny would relieve her. Thus, in accordance with Mr. Trelawny's instructions, there would always be a man and a woman in the room; and each one of us would overlap, so that at no time would a new set of watchers come on duty without some one to tell of what—if anything—had occurred. I lay down on a sofa in my own room, having arranged that one of the servants should call me a little before twelve. In a few moments I was asleep.

When I was waked, it took me several seconds to get back my thoughts so as to recognize my own identity and surroundings. The short sleep had, however, done me good, and I could look on things around me in a more practical light than I had been able to do earlier in the evening. I bathed my face, and thus refreshed went into the sick-room. I moved very softly. The Nurse was sitting by the bed, quiet and alert; the Detective sat in an arm-chair across the room in deep shadow. He did not move when I crossed, until I got close to him, when he said in a dull whisper:

"It is all right; I have not been asleep!" An unnecessary thing to say, I thought—it always is, unless it be untrue in spirit. When I told him that his watch was over; that he might go to bed till I should call him at six o'clock, he seemed relieved and went with alacrity. At the door he turned and, coming back to me, said in a whisper:

"I sleep lightly and I shall have my pistols with me. I won't feel so heavy-headed when I get out of this mummy smell."

He too, then, had shared my experience of drowsiness!

I asked the Nurse if she wanted anything. I noticed that she had a vinaigrette in her lap. Doubtless she, too, had felt some of the influence which had so affected me. She said that she had all she required, but that if she should want anything she would at once let me know. I wished to keep her from noticing my respirator, so I went to the chair in the shadow where her back was toward me. Here I quietly put it on, and made myself comfortable.

For what seemed a long time, I sat and thought and thought. It was a wild medley of thoughts, as might have been expected from the experiences of the previous day and night. Again I found myself thinking of the Egyptian smell; and I remember that I felt a delicious satisfaction that I did not experience it as I had done. The respirator was doing its work.

It must have been that the passing of this disturbing thought made for repose of mind, which is the corollary of bodily rest, for, though I really cannot remember being asleep or waking from it, I saw a vision—I dreamed a dream, I scarcely know which.

I was still in the room, seated in the chair. I had on my respirator and knew that I breathed freely. The Nurse sat in her chair with her back toward me. She sat quite still. The sick man lay as still as the dead. It was rather like the picture of a scene than the reality; all were still and silent; and the stillness and silence were continuous. Outside, in the distance I could hear the sounds of a city, the occasional roll of wheels, the shout of a reveler, the far-away echo of whistles and the rumbling of trains. The light was very, very low; the reflection of it under the green-shaded lamp was a dim relief to the darkness, rather than light. The green silk fringe of the lamp had merely the color of an emerald seen in the moon-light. The room, for all its darkness, was full of shadows. It seemed in my whirling thoughts as though all the real things had become shadows—shadows which moved, for they passed the dim outline of the high windows. Shadows which had sentience. I even thought there was sound, a faint sound as of the mew of a cat—the rustle of drapery and a metallic clink as of metal faintly touching metal. I sat as one entranced. At last I felt, as in nightmare, that this was sleep, and that in the passing of its portals all my will had gone.

All at once my senses were full awake. A shriek rang in my ears. The room was filled suddenly with a blaze of light. There was the sound of pistol shots—one, two; and a haze of white smoke in the room. When my waking eyes regained their power, I could have shrieked with horror myself at what I saw before me.

The Cats of Ulthar

[H. P. LOVECRAFT]

It is said that in Ulthar, which lies beyond the river Skai, no man may kill a cat; and this I can verily believe as I gaze upon him who sitteth purring before the fire. For the cat is cryptic, and close to strange things which men cannot see. He is the soul of antique Aegyptus, and bearer of tales from forgotten cities in Meroe and Ophir. He is the kin of the jungle's lords, and heir to the secrets of hoary and sinister Africa. The Sphinx is his cousin, and he speaks her language; but he is more ancient than the Sphinx, and remembers that which she hath forgotten.

In Ulthar, before ever the burgesses forbade the killing of cats, there dwelt an old cotter and his wife who delighted to trap and slay the cats of their neighbors. Why they did this I know not; save that many hate the voice of the cat in the night, and take it ill that cats should run stealthily about yards and gardens at twilight. But whatever the reason, this old man and woman took pleasure in trapping and slaying every cat which came near to their hovel; and from some of the sounds heard after dark, many villagers fancied that the manner of slaying was exceedingly peculiar. But the villagers did not discuss such things with the old man and his wife; because of the habitual expression on the withered faces of the two, and because their cottage was so small and so darkly hidden under spreading oaks at the back of a neglected yard. In truth, much as the owners of cats hated these odd folk, they feared them more; and instead of berating them as brutal assassins, merely took care that no cherished pet or mouser should stray toward the remote hovel under the dark trees. When through some unavoidable oversight a cat was missed, and sounds heard after dark, the loser would lament impotently; or console himself by thanking Fate that it was not one of his children who had thus vanished. For the people of Ulthar were simple, and knew not whence it is all cats first came.

One day a caravan of strange wanderers from the South entered the narrow, cobbled streets of Ulthar. Dark wanderers they were, and unlike the other roving folk who passed through the village twice every year. In the market-place they told fortunes for silver, and bought gay beads from the merchants. What was the land of these wanderers none could tell; but it was seen that they were given to strange prayers, and that they had painted on the sides of their wagons strange figures with human bodies and the heads of cats, hawks, rams, and lions. And the leader of the caravan wore a headdress with two horns and a curious disk betwixt the horns.

There was in this singular caravan a little boy with no father or mother, but only a tiny black kitten to cherish. The plague had not been kind to him, yet had left him this small furry thing to mitigate his sorrow; and when one is very young, one can find great relief in the lively antics of a black kitten. So the boy whom the dark people called Menes smiled more often than he wept as he sat playing with his graceful kitten on the steps of an oddly painted wagon.

On the third morning of the wanderers' stay in Ulthar, Menes could not find his kitten; and as he sobbed aloud in the market-place certain villagers told him of the old man and his wife, and of sounds heard in the night. And when he heard these things his sobbing gave place to meditation, and finally to prayer. He stretched out his arms toward the sun and prayed in a tongue no villager could understand; though indeed the villagers did not try very hard to understand, since their attention was mostly taken up by the sky and the odd shapes the clouds were assuming. It was very peculiar, but as the little boy uttered his petition there seemed to form overhead the shadowy, nebulous figures of exotic things; of hybrid creatures crowned with horn-flanked disks. Nature is full of such illusions to impress the imaginative.

That night the wanderers left Ulthar, and were never seen again. And the householders were troubled when they noticed that in all the village there was not a cat to be found. From each hearth the familiar cat had vanished; cats large and small, black, grey, striped, yellow, and white. Old Kranon, the burgomaster, swore that the dark folk had taken the cats away in revenge for the killing of Menes' kitten; and cursed the caravan and the little boy. But Nith, the lean notary, declared that the old cotter and his wife were more likely persons to suspect; for their hatred of cats was notorious and increasingly bold. Still, no one durst complain to the sinister couple; even when little Atal, the innkeeper's son, vowed that he had at twilight seen all the cats of Ulthar in that accursed yard under the trees, pacing very slowly and solemnly in a circle around the cottage, two abreast, as if in performance of some unheard-of rite of beasts. The villagers did not know how much to believe from so small a boy; and though they feared that the evil pair had charmed the cats to their death, they preferred not to chide the old cotter till they met him outside his dark and repellent yard.

So Ulthar went to sleep in vain anger, and when the people awakened at dawn—behold! every cat was back at his accustomed hearth! Large and small, black, grey, striped, yellow, and white, none was missing. Very sleek and fat did the cats appear, and sonorous with purring content. The citizens talked with one another of the affair, and marveled not a little. Old Kranon again insisted that it was the dark folk who had taken them, since cats did not return alive from the cottage of the ancient man and his wife. But all agreed on one thing: that the refusal of all the cats to eat their portions of meat or drink their saucers of milk was exceedingly curious. And for two whole days the sleek, lazy cats of Ulthar would touch no food, but only doze by the fire or in the sun.

It was fully a week before the villagers noticed that no lights were appearing at dusk in the windows of the cottage under the trees. Then the lean Nith remarked that no one had seen the old man or his wife since the night the cats were away. In another week the burgomaster decided to overcome his fears and call at the strangely silent dwelling as a matter of duty, though in so doing he was careful to take with him Shang the blacksmith and Thul the cutter of stone as witnesses. And when they had broken down the frail door they found only this: two cleanly picked human skeletons on the earthen floor, and a number of singular beetles crawling in the shadowy corners.

There was subsequently much talk among the burgesses of Ulthar. Zath, the coroner, disputed at length with Nith, the lean notary; and Kranon and Shang and Thul were overwhelmed with questions. Even little Atal, the innkeeper's son, was closely questioned and given a sweetmeat as reward. They talked of the old cotter and his wife, of the caravan of dark wanderers, of small Menes and his black kitten, of the prayer of Menes and of the sky during that prayer, of the doings of the cats on the night the caravan left, and of what was later found in the cottage under the dark trees in the repellent yard.

And in the end the burgesses passed that remarkable law which is told of by traders in Hatheg and discussed by travelers in Nir; namely, that in Ulthar no man may kill a cat.

The Empty Sleeve

[ALGERNON BLACKWOOD]

I

The Gilmer brothers were a couple of fussy and pernickety old bachelors of a rather retiring, not to say timid, disposition. There was gray in the pointed beard of John, the elder, and if any hair had remained to William it would also certainly have been of the same shade. They had private means. Their main interest in life was the collection of violins, for which they had the instinctive *flair* of true connoisseurs. Neither John nor William, however, could play a single note. They could only pluck the open strings. The production of tone, so necessary before the purchase was done vicariously for them by another.

The only objection they had to the big building in which they occupied the roomy top floor was that Morgan, liftman and caretaker, insisted on wearing a billycock with his uniform after six o'clock in the evening, with a result disastrous to the beauty of the universe. For "Mr. Morgan," as they called him between themselves, had a round and pasty face on the top of a round and conical body. In view, however, of the man's other rare qualities—including his devotion to themselves—this objection was not serious.

He had another peculiarity that amused them. On being found fault with, explained nothing, but merely repeated the words of the complaint.

"Water in the bath wasn't really hot this morning, Morgan!"

"Water in the bath reely 'ot, wasn't it, sir?"

Or, from William, who was something of a faddist:

"My jar of sour milk came up late yesterday, Morgan."

"Your jar of sour milk come up late, sir, yesterday?"

Since, however, the statement of a complaint invariably resulted in its remedy, the brothers had learned to look for no further explanation. Next morning the bath *was* hot, the sour milk *was* "brortup" punctually. The uniform and billycock hat, though, remained an eyesore and source of oppression.

On this particular night John Gilmer, the elder, returning from a Masonic rehearsal, stepped into the lift and found Mr. Morgan with his hand ready on the iron rope.

"Fog's very thick outside," said Mr. John pleasantly; and the lift was a third of the way up before Morgan had completed his customary repetition: "Fog very thick outside, yes, sir." And Gilmer then asked casually if his brother were alone, and received the reply that Mr. Hyman had called and had not yet gone away.

Now this Mr. Hyman was a Hebrew, and, like themselves, a connoisseur in violins, but, unlike themselves, who only kept their specimens to look at, he was a skillful and exquisite player. He was the only person they ever permitted to handle their pedigree instruments, to take them from the glass cases where they reposed in silent splendor, and to draw the sound out of their wondrous painted hearts of golden varnish. The brothers loathed to see his fingers touch them, yet loved to hear their singing voices in the room, for the latter confirmed their sound judgment as collectors, and made them certain their money had been well spent. Hyman, however, made no attempt to conceal his contempt and hatred for the mere collectors. The atmosphere of the room fairly pulsed with these opposing forces of silent emotion when Hyman played and the Gilmers, alternately writhing and admiring, listened. The occasions, however, were not frequent. The

Hebrew only came by invitation, and both brothers made a point of being in. It was a very formal proceeding—something of a sacred rite almost.

John Gilmer, therefore, was considerably surprised by the information Morgan had supplied. For one thing, Hyman, he had understood, was away on the Continent.

"Still in there, you say?" he repeated, after a moment's reflection.

"Still in there, Mr. John, sir." Then, concealing his surprise from the liftman, he fell back upon his usual mild habit of complaining about the billycock hat and the uniform.

"You really should try and remember, Morgan," he said, though kindly. "That hat does not go well with that uniform!"

Morgan's pasty countenance betrayed no vestige of expression.

"At don't go well with the yewniform, sir," he repeated, hanging up the disreputable bowler and replacing it with a gold-braided cap from the peg. "No, sir, it don't, do it?" he added cryptically, smiling at the transformation thus effected.

And the lift then halted with an abrupt jerk at the top floor. By somebody's carelessness the landing was in darkness, and, to make things worse, Morgan, clumsily pulling the iron rope, happened to knock the billycock from its peg so that his sleeve, as he stooped to catch it, struck the switch and plunged the scene in a moment's complete obscurity.

And it was then, in the act of stepping out before the light was turned on again, that John Gilmer stumbled against something that shot along the landing past the open door. First he thought it must be a child, then a man, then—an animal. Its movement was rapid yet stealthy. Starting backwards instinctively to allow it room to pass, Gilmer collided in the darkness with Morgan, and Morgan incontinently screamed. There was a moment of stupid confusion. The heavy framework of the lift shook a little, as though something had stepped into it and then as quickly jumped out again. A rushing sound followed that resembled footsteps, yet at the same time was more like gliding—someone in soft slippers or stockinged feet, greatly hurrying. Then came silence again. Morgan sprang to the landing and turned up the electric light. Mr. Gilmer, at the same moment, did likewise to the switch in the lift. Light flooded the scene. Nothing was visible.

"Dog or cat, or something, I suppose, wasn't it?" exclaimed Gilmer, following the man out and looking round with bewildered amazement upon a deserted landing. He knew quite well, even while he spoke, that the words were foolish.

"Dog or cat, yes, sir, or—something," echoed Morgan, his eyes narrowed to pin-points, then growing large, but his face stolid.

"The light should have been on," Mr. Gilmer spoke with a touch of severity. The little occurrence had curiously disturbed his equanimity. He felt annoyed, upset, uneasy.

For a perceptible pause the liftman made no reply, and his employer, looking up, saw that, besides being flustered, he was white about the jaws. His voice, when he spoke, was without its normal assurance. This time he did not merely repeat. He explained.

"The light *was* on, sir, when last *I* come up!" he said, with emphasis, obviously speaking the truth. "Only a moment ago," he added.

Mr. Gilmer, for some reason, felt disinclined to press for explanations. He decided to ignore the matter.

Then the lift plunged down again into the depths like a diving-bell into water; and John Gilmer, pausing a moment first to reflect, let himself in softly with his latchkey, and, after hanging up hat and coat in the hall, entered the big sitting room he and his brother shared in common.

The December fog that covered London like a dirty blanket had penetrated, he saw, into the room. The objects in it were half shrouded in the familiar yellowish haze.

II

In his dressing-gown and slippers, William Gilmer, almost invisible in his armchair by the gas-stove across the room, spoke at once. Through the thick atmosphere his face gleamed, showing an extinguished pipe hanging from his lips. His tone of voice conveyed emotion, an emotion he sought to suppress, of a quality, however, not easy to define.

"Hyman's been here," he announced abruptly. "You must have met him. He's this very instant gone out."

It was quite easy to see that something had happened, for "scenes" leave disturbance behind them in the atmosphere. But John made no immediate reference to this. He replied that he had seen no one— which was strictly true—and his brother thereupon, sitting bolt upright in the chair, turned quickly and faced him. His skin, in the foggy air, seemed paler than before.

"That's odd," he said nervously.

"What's odd?" asked John.

"That you didn't see—anything. You ought to have run into one another on the doorstep." His eyes went peering about the room. He was distinctly ill at ease. "You're positive you saw no one? Did Morgan take him down before you came? Did Morgan see him?" He asked several questions at once.

"On the contrary, Morgan told me he was still here with you. Hyman probably walked down, and didn't take the lift at all," he replied. "That accounts for neither of us seeing him." He decided to say nothing about the occurrence in the lift, for his brother's nerves, he saw plainly, were on edge.

William then stood up out of his chair, and the skin of his face changed its hue, for whereas a moment ago it was merely pale, it had now altered to a tint that lay somewhere between white and a livid gray. The man was fighting internal terror. For a moment these two brothers of middle age looked each other straight in the eye. Then John spoke:

"What's wrong, Billy?" he asked quietly. "Something's upset you. What brought Hyman in this way—unexpectedly? I thought he was still in Germany."

The brothers, affectionate and sympathetic, understood one another perfectly. They had no secrets. Yet for several minutes the younger one made no reply. It seemed difficult to choose his words apparently.

"Hyman played, I suppose—on the fiddles?" John helped him, wondering uneasily what was coming. He did not care much for the individual in question, though his talent was of such great use to them.

The other nodded in the affirmative, then plunged into rapid speech, talking under his breath as though he feared someone might overhear. Glancing over his shoulder down the foggy room, he drew his brother close.

"Hyman came," he began, "unexpectedly. He hadn't written, and I hadn't asked him. You hadn't either, I suppose?"

John shook his head.

"When I came in from the dining-room I found him in the passage. The servant was taking away the dishes, and he had let himself in while the front door was ajar. Pretty cool, wasn't it?"

"He's an original," said John, shrugging his shoulders. "And you welcomed him?" he asked.

"I asked him in, of course. He explained he had something glorious for me to hear. Silenski had played it in the afternoon, and he had bought the music since. But Silenski's 'Strad' hadn't the power—it's thin on the upper strings, you remember, unequal, patchy—and he said no instrument in the world could do it justice but our 'Joseph'—the small Guarnerius, you know, which he swears is the most perfect in the world."

"And what was it? Did he play it?" asked John, growing more uneasy as he grew more interested. With relief he glanced round and saw the matchless little instrument lying there safe and sound in its glass case near the door.

"He played it—divinely: Zigeuner Lullaby, a fine, passionate, rushing bit of inspiration, oddly-misnamed 'lullaby.' And, fancy the fellow had memorized it already! He walked about the room on tiptoe while he played it, complaining of the light—"

"Complaining of the light?"

"Said the thing was crepuscular, and needed dusk for its full effect. I turned the lights out one by one, till finally there was only the glow of the gas logs. He insisted. You know that way he has with him? And then he got over me in another matter: insisted on using some special strings he had brought with him, and put them on, too, himself—thicker than the A and E *we* use."

For though neither Gilmer could produce a note, it was their pride that they kept their precious instruments in perfect condition for playing, choosing the exact thickness and quality of strings that suited the temperament of each violin; and the little Guarnerius in question always "sang" best, they held, with thin strings.

"Infernal insolence," exclaimed the listening brother, wondering what was coming next. "Played it well, though, didn't he, this Lullaby thing?" he added, seeing that William hesitated. As he spoke he went nearer, sitting down close beside him in a leather chair.

"Magnificent! Pure fire of genius!" was the reply with enthusiasm, the voice at the same time dropping lower. "Staccato like a silver hammer; harmonics like flutes, clear, soft, ringing; and the tone—well, the G string was a baritone, and the upper registers creamy and mellow as a boy's voice. John," he added, "that Guarnerius is the very pick of the period and"— again he hesitated—"Hyman loves it. He'd give his soul to have it."

The more John heard, the more uncomfortable it made him. He had always disliked this gifted Hebrew, for in his secret heart he knew that he had always feared and distrusted him. Sometimes he had felt half afraid of him; the man's very forcible personality was too insistent to be pleasant. His type was of the dark and sinister kind, and he possessed a violent will that rarely failed of accomplishing its desire.

"Wish I'd heard the fellow play," he said at length, ignoring his brother's last remark, and going on to speak of the most matter-of-fact details he could think of. "Did he use the Dodd bow, or the Tourte? That Dodd I picked up last month, you know, is the most perfectly balanced I have ever—"

He stopped abruptly, for William had suddenly got upon his feet and was standing there, searching the room with his eyes. A chill ran down John's spine as he watched him.

"What is it, Billy?" he asked sharply. "Hear anything?"

William continued to peer about him through the thick air.

"Oh, nothing, probably," he said, an odd catch in his voice; "only—I keep feeling as if there was somebody listening. Do you think, perhaps"—he glanced over his shoulder—"there is someone at the door? I wish—I wish you'd have a look, John."

John obeyed, though without great eagerness. Crossing the room slowly, he opened the door, then switched on the light. The passage leading past the bathroom towards the bedrooms beyond was empty. The coats hung motionless from their pegs.

"No one, of course," he said, as he closed the door and came back to the stove. He left the light burning in the passage. It was curious the way both brothers had this impression that they were not alone, though only one of them spoke of it.

"Used the Dodd or the Tourte, Billy—which?" continued John in the most natural voice he could assume.

But at that very same instant the water started to his eyes. His brother, he saw, was close upon the thing he really had to tell. But he had stuck fast.

III

By a great effort John Gilmer composed himself and remained in his chair. With detailed elaboration he lit a cigarette, staring hard at his brother over the flaring match while he did so. There he sat in his dressing-gown and slippers by the fireplace, eyes downcast, fingers playing idly with the red tassel. The electric light cast heavy shadows across the face. In a flash then, since emotion may sometimes express itself in attitude even better than in speech, the elder brother understood that Billy was about to tell him an unutterable thing.

By instinct he moved over to his side so that the same view of the room confronted him.

"Out with it, old man," he said, with an effort to be natural. "Tell me what you saw."

Billy shuffled slowly round and the two sat side by side, facing the fog-draped chamber.

"It was like this," he began softly, "only I was standing instead of sitting, looking over to that door as you and I do now. Hyman moved to and fro in the faint glow of the gas logs against the far wall, playing the 'crepuscular' thing in his most inspired sort of way, so that the music seemed to issue from himself rather than from the shining bit of wood under his chin, when—I noticed something coming over me that was"—he hesitated, searching for words—"that wasn't *all* due to the music," he finished abruptly.

"His personality put a bit of hypnotism on you, eh?"

William shrugged his shoulders.

"The air was thickish with fog and the light was dim, cast upwards upon him from the stove," he continued. "I admit all that. But there wasn't light enough to throw shadows, you see, and—"

"Hyman looked queer?" the other helped him quickly.

Billy nodded his head without turning.

"Changed there before my very eyes"—he whispered it—"turned animal—"

"Animal?" John felt his hair rising.

"That's the only way I can put it. His face and hands and body turned otherwise than usual. I lost the sound of his feet. When the bow-hand or the fingers on the strings passed into the light, they were"—he uttered a soft, shuddering little laugh—"furry, oddly divided, the fingers massed together. And he paced stealthily. I thought every instant the fiddle would drop with a crash and he would spring at me across the room."

"My dear chap—"

"He moved with those big, lithe, striding steps one sees"—John held his breath in the little pause, listening keenly—"one sees those big brutes make in the cages when their desire is aflame for food or escape, or—or fierce passionate desire for anything they want with their whole nature—"

"The big felines!" John whistled softly.

"And every minute getting nearer and nearer to the door, as though he meant to make a sudden rush for it and get out."

"With the violin! Of course you stopped him?"

"In the end. But for a long time, I swear to you, I found it difficult to know what to do, even to move. I couldn't get my voice for words of any kind; it was like a spell."

"It *was* a spell," suggested John firmly.

"Then, as he moved, still playing," continued the other, "he seemed to grow smaller; to shrink down below the line of the gas. I thought I should lose sight of him altogether. I turned the light up suddenly. There he was over by the door—crouching."

"Playing on his knees, you mean?"

William closed his eyes in an effort to visualize it again.

"Crouching," he repeated, at length, "close to the floor. At least, I think so. It all happened so quickly, and I felt so bewildered, it was hard to see straight. But at first I could have sworn he was half his natural size. I called to him, I think I swore at him—I forget exactly, but I know he straightened up at once and stood before me down there in the light"—he pointed across the room to the door—"eyes gleaming, face white as chalk, perspiring like midsummer, and gradually filling out, straightening up, whatever you like to call it, to his natural size and appearance again. It was the most horrid thing I've ever seen."

"As an—animal, you saw him still?"

"No; human again. Only much smaller."

"What did he say?"

Billy reflected a moment.

"Nothing that I can remember," he replied. "You see, it was all over in a few seconds. In the full light, I felt so foolish, and nonplused at first. To see him normal again baffled me. And, before I could collect myself, he had let himself out into the passage, and I heard the front door slam. A minute later—the same second almost, it seemed—you came in. I only remember grabbing the violin and getting it back safely under the glass case. The strings were still vibrating."

The account was over. John asked no further questions. Nor did he say a single word about the lift, Morgan, or the extinguished light on the landing. There fell a longish silence between the two men; and then, while they helped themselves to a generous supply of whisky-and-soda before going to bed, John looked up and spoke:

"If you agree, Billy," he said quietly, "I think I might write and suggest to Hyman that we shall no longer have need for his services."

And Billy, acquiescing, added a sentence that expressed something of the singular dread lying but half-concealed in the atmosphere of the room, if not in their minds as well:

"Putting it, however, in a way that need not offend him."

"Of course. There's no need to be rude, is there?"

Accordingly, next morning the letter was written; and John, saying nothing to his brother, took it round himself by hand to the Hebrew's rooms near Euston. The answer he dreaded was forthcoming:

"Mr. Hyman's still away abroad," he was told. "But we're forwarding letters; yes. Or I can give you his address if you'll prefer it." The letter went, therefore, to the number in Konigstrasse, Munich, thus obtained.

Then, on his way back from the insurance company where he went to increase the sum that protected the small Guarnerius from loss by fire, accident, or theft, John Gilmer called at the offices of certain musical agents and ascertained that Silenski, the violinist, was performing at the time in Munich. It was only some days later, though, by diligent inquiry, he made certain that at a concert on a certain date the famous virtuoso had played a Zigeuner Lullaby of his own composition—the very date, it turned out, on which he himself had been to the Masonic rehearsal at Mark Masons' Hall.

John, however, said nothing of these discoveries to his brother William.

IV

It was about a week later when a reply to the letter came from Munich—a letter couched in somewhat offensive terms, though it contained neither words nor phrases that could actually be found fault with. Isidore Hyman was hurt and angry. On his return to London a month or so later, he proposed to call and talk the matter over. The offensive part of the letter, lay, perhaps, in his definite assumption that he could persuade the brothers to resume the old relations. John, however, wrote a brief reply to the effect that they had decided to buy no new fiddles; their collection being complete, there would be no occasion for them to invite his services as a performer. This was final. No answer came, and the matter seemed to drop. Never for one moment, though, did it leave the consciousness of John Gilmer. Hyman had said that he would come, and come assuredly he would. He secretly gave Morgan instructions that he and his brother for the future were always "out" when Hyman presented himself.

"He must have gone back to Germany, you see, almost at once after his visit here that night," observed William—John, however, making no reply.

One night towards the middle of January the two brothers came home together from a concert in Queen's Hall, and sat up later than usual in their sitting-room discussing over their whisky and tobacco the merits of the pieces and performers. It must have been past one o'clock when they turned out the lights in the passage and retired to bed. The air was still and frosty; moonlight over the roofs—one of those sharp and dry winter nights that now seem to visit London rarely.

"Like the old-fashioned days when we were boys," remarked William, pausing a moment by the passage window and looking out across the miles of silvery, sparkling roofs.

"Yes," added John; "the ponds freezing hard in the fields, rime on the nursery windows, and the sound of a horse's hoofs coming down the road in the distance, eh?" They smiled at the memory, then said good night, and separated. Their rooms were at opposite ends of the corridor; in between were the bathroom, dining-room, and sitting-room. It was a long, straggling flat. Half an hour later both brothers were sound asleep, the flat silent, only a dull murmur rising from the great city outside, and the moon sinking slowly to the level of the chimneys.

Perhaps two hours passed, perhaps three, when John Gilmer, sitting up in bed with a start, wide-awake and frightened, knew that someone was moving about in one of the three rooms that lay between him and his brother. He had absolutely no idea why he should have been frightened, for there was no dream or nightmare-memory that he brought over from unconsciousness. And yet he realized plainly that the fear he felt was by no means a foolish and unreasoning fear. It had a cause and a reason. Also—which made it worse—it was fully warranted. Something in his sleep, forgotten in the instant of waking, had happened that set every nerve in his body on the watch. He was positive only of two things—first, that it was the entrance of this person, moving so quietly there in the flat, that sent the chills down his spine; and, secondly, that this person was *not* his brother William.

John Gilmer was a timid man. The sight of a burglar, his eyes black-masked, suddenly confronting him in the passage, would most likely have deprived him of all power of decision—until the burglar had either shot him or escaped. But on this occasion some instinct told him that it was no burglar, and that the acute distress he experienced was not due to any message of ordinary physical fear. The thing that had gained access to his flat while he slept had first come—he felt sure of it—into his room, and had passed very close to his own bed, before going on. It had then doubtless gone to his brother's room, visiting them both stealthily to make sure they slept. And its mere passage through his room had been enough to wake him and set these drops of cold perspiration upon his skin. For it was—he felt it in every fiber of his body—something hostile.

The thought that it might at that very moment be in the room of his brother, however, brought him to his feet on the cold floor, and set him moving with all the determination he could summon towards the door. He looked cautiously down an utterly dark passage; then crept on tiptoe along it. On the wall were old-fashioned weapons that had belonged to his father; and feeling a curved, sheathless sword that had come from some Turkish campaign of years gone by, his fingers closed tightly round it, and lifted it silently from the three hooks whereon it lay. He passed the doors of the bathroom and dining-room, making instinctively for the big sitting-room where the violins were kept in their glass cases. The cold nipped him. His eyes smarted with the effort to see in the darkness. Outside the closed door he hesitated.

Putting his ear to the crack, he listened. From within came a faint sound of someone moving. The same instant there rose the sharp, delicate "ping" of a violin-string being plucked; and John Gilmer, with nerves that shook like the vibrations of that very string, opened the door wide with a fling and turned on the light at the same moment. The plucked string still echoed faintly in the air.

The sensation that met him on the threshold was the well-known one that things had been going on in the room which his unexpected arrival had that instant put a stop to. A second earlier and he would have discovered it all in the act. The atmosphere still held the feeling of rushing, silent movement with which the things had raced back to their normal, motionless positions. The immobility of the furniture was a mere attitude hurriedly assumed, and the moment his back was turned the whole business, whatever it might be, would begin again. With this presentment of the room—however—a purely imaginative one, came another, swiftly on its heels.

For one of the objects, less swift than the rest, had not quite regained its "attitude" of repose. It still moved. Below the window curtains on the right, not far from the shelf that bore the violins in their glass cases, he made it out, slowly gliding along the floor. Then, even as his eye caught it, it came to rest.

And, while the cold perspiration broke out all over him afresh, he knew that this still moving item was the cause both of his waking and of his terror. This was the disturbance whose presence he had divined in the flat without actual hearing, and whose passage through his room, while he yet slept, had touched every nerve in his body as with ice. Clutching his Turkish sword tightly, he drew back with the utmost caution against the wall and watched, for the singular impression came to him that the movement was not that of a human being crouching, but rather of something that pertained to the animal world. He remembered, flash-like, the movements of reptiles, the stealth of the larger felines, the undulating glide of great snakes. For the moment, however, it did not move, and they faced one another.

The other side of the room was but dimly lighted, and the noise he made clicking up another electric lamp brought the thing flying forward again—towards himself. At such a moment it seemed absurd to think of so small a detail, but he remembered his bare feet, and, genuinely frightened, he leaped upon a chair and swished with his sword though the air about him. From this better point of view, with the increased light to aid him, he then saw two things—first, that the glass case usually covering the Guarnerius violin had been shifted; and, secondly, that the moving object was slowly elongating itself into an upright position. Semi-erect, yet most oddly, too, like a creature on its hind legs, it was coming swiftly towards him. It was making for the door—and escape.

The confusion of ghostly fear was somehow upon him so that he was too bewildered to see clearly, but he had sufficient control, it seemed, to recover a certain power of action; for the moment the advancing figure was near enough for him to strike, that curved scimitar flashed and whirred about him, with such misdirected violence, however, that he not only failed to strike it even once, but at the same time lost his balance and fell forward from the chair whereon he perched—straight into it.

And then came the most curious thing of all, for as he dropped, the figure also dropped, stooped low down, crouched, dwindled amazingly in size, and rushed past him close to the ground like an animal on all fours. John Gilmer screamed, for he could no longer contain himself. Stumbling over the chair as he turned to follow, cutting and slashing wildly with his sword, he saw half-way down the darkened corridor beyond the scuttling outline of, apparently, an enormous—cat!

The door into the outer landing was somehow ajar, and the next second the beast was out, but not before the steel had fallen with a crashing blow upon the front disappearing leg, almost severing it from the body.

It was dreadful. Turning up the lights as he went, he ran after it to the outer landing. But the thing he followed was already well away, and he heard, on the floor below him, the same oddly gliding, slithering, stealthy sound, yet hurrying, that he heard weeks before when something had passed him in the lift, and Morgan, in his terror, had likewise cried aloud.

For a time he stood there on that dark landing, listening, thinking, trembling; then turned into the flat and shut the door. In the sitting-room he carefully replaced the glass case over the treasured violin, puzzled to the point of foolishness, and strangely routed in his mind. For the violin itself, he saw, had been dragged several inches from its cushioned bed of plush.

Next morning, however, he made no allusion to the occurrence of the night. His brother apparently had not been disturbed.

V

The only thing that called for explanation—an explanation not fully forthcoming—was the curious aspect of Mr. Morgan's countenance. The fact that this individual gave notice to the owners of the building, and at the end of the month left for a new post, was, of course, known to both brothers; whereas the story he told in explanation of his face was known only to the one who questioned him about it—John. And John, for reasons best known to himself, did not pass it on to the other. Also, for reasons best known to himself, he did not cross-question the liftman about those singular marks, or report the matter to the police.

Mr. Morgan's pasty visage was badly scratched, and there were red lines running from the cheek into the neck that had the appearance of having been produced by sharp points viciously applied—claws. He had been disturbed by a noise in the hall, he said, about three in the morning. A scuffle had ensued in the darkness, but the intruder had got clear away. . . .

"A cat, or something of the kind, no doubt," suggested John Gilmer at the end of the brief recital.

And Morgan replied in his usual way: "A cat, or something of the kind, Mr. John, no doubt."

All the same, he had not cared to risk a second encounter, but had departed to wear his billycock and uniform in a building less haunted.

Hyman, meanwhile, made no attempt to call and talk over his dismissal. The reason for this was only apparent, however, several months later when, quite by chance, coming along Piccadilly in an omnibus, the brothers found themselves seated opposite to a man with a thick black beard and blue glasses. William Gilmer hastily rang the bell and got out, saying something half intelligible about feeling faint. John followed him.

"Did you see who it was?" he whispered to his brother the moment they were safely on the pavement.

John nodded.

"Hyman, in spectacles. He's grown a beard, too."

"Yes, but didn't you also notice—"

"What?"

"He had an empty sleeve."

"An empty sleeve?"

"Yes," said William; "he's lost an arm."

There was a long pause before John spoke. At the door of their club the elder brother added:

"Poor devil! He'll never again play on"—then, suddenly changing the preposition—"*with* a pedigree violin!" And that night in the flat, after William had gone to bed, he looked up a curious old volume he had once picked up on a secondhand bookstall, and read therein quaint descriptions of how the "desire-body of a violent man" may assume animal shape, operate on concrete matter even at a distance; and, further, how a wound inflicted thereon can reproduce itself upon its physical counterpart by means of the mysterious so-called phenomenon of "re-percussion."

The Cat of the Cane-Brake

[FREDERICK STUART GREENE]

"Sally! O-oh, Sally! I'm a-goin' now." Jim Gantt pushed back the limp brim of his rusty felt hat and turned colorless eyes toward the cabin.

A young woman came from around the corner of the house. From each hand dangled a bunch of squawking chickens. She did not speak until she had reached the wagon.

"Now, Jim, you ain't a-goin' to let them fellers down in Andalushy git you inter no blind tiger, air you?" The question came in a hopeless drawl; hopeless, too, her look into the man's sallow face.

"I ain't tetched a drop in more'n three months, has I?" Jim's answer was in a sullen key.

"No, Jim, you bin doin' right well lately." She tossed the chickens into the wagon, thoughtless of the hurt to their tied and twisted legs. "They're worth two bits apiece. That comes to two dollars, Jim. Don't you take a nickel less'n that."

Jim gave a listless pull at the cotton rope that served as reins.

"Git up thar, mule!" he called, and the wagon creaked off on wobbling wheels down the hot, dusty road.

The woman looked scornfully at the man's humped-over back for a full minute, turned and walked to the house, a hard smile at her mouth.

Sally Gantt gave no heed to her drab surroundings as she crossed the short stretch from road to cabin. All her twenty-two years had been spent in this far end of Alabama, where one dreary, unkempt clearing in the pine-woods is as dismal as the next. Comparisons which might add their fuel to her smoldering discontent were spared her. Yet, unconsciously, this bare, grassless country, with its flat miles of monotonous pine forests, its flatter miles of rank cane-brake, served to distil gall, poisoning all her thoughts.

The double cabin of Jim Gantt, its two rooms separated by a "dog-trot"—an open porch cut through the center of the structure—was counted a thing of luxury by his scattered neighbors. Gantt had built it four years before, when he took up the land as his homestead, and Sally for his wife. The labor of building this cabin had apparently drained his stock of energy to the dregs. Beyond the necessary toil of planting a small patch of corn, a smaller one of sweet potatoes, and fishing in the sluggish waters of Pigeon Creek, he now did nothing. Sally tended the chickens, their one source of money, and gave intermittent attention to the half-dozen razor-back hogs, which, with the scrubby mule, comprises their toll of live-stock.

As the woman mounted the hewn log that answered as a step to the dog-trot, she stopped to listen. From the kitchen came a faint noise; a sound of crunching. Sally went on silent feet to the door. On the table, littered with unwashed dishes, a cat was gnawing at a fish head—a gaunt beast, its lean flanks covered with wiry fur except where ragged scars left exposed the bare hide. Its strong jaws crushed through the thick skull-bone of the fish as if it were an empty bird's egg.

Sally sprang to the stove and seized a pine knot.

"Dog-gone your yaller hide!" she screamed. "Git out of hyar!"

The cat wheeled with a start and faced the woman, its evil eyes glittering.

"Git, you yaller devil!" the woman screamed again.

The cat sprang sidewise to the floor. Sally sent the jagged piece of wood spinning through the air. It crashed against the far wall, missing the beast by an inch. The animal arched its huge body and held its ground.

"You varmint, I'll git you this time!" Sally stooped for another piece of wood. The cat darted through the door ahead of the flying missile.

"I'll kill you yit!" Sally shouted after it. "An' he kain't hinder me neither!"

She sat down heavily and wiped the sweat from her forehead.

It was several minutes before the woman rose from the chair and crossed the dog-trot to the sleeping-room. Throwing her faded sunbonnet into a corner, she loosened her hair and began to brush it.

Sally Gantt was neither pretty nor handsome. But in a country peopled solely by pinewoods crackers, her black hair and eyes, clear skin and white teeth, made her stand out. She was a woman, and young. To a man, also young, who for two years had seen no face unpainted with the sallow hue of chills and fever, no eyes except faded blue ones framed by white, straggling lashes, no sound teeth, and the unsound ones stained always by the snuff stick, she might easily appear alluring.

With feminine deftness Sally re-coiled her hair. She took from a wooden peg a blue calico dress, its printed pattern as yet unbleached by the fierce suns. It gave to her slender figure some touch of grace. From beneath the bed she drew a pair of heavy brogans; a shoe fashioned, doubtless, to match the listless nature of the people who most use them, slipping on or off without hindrance from lace or buckle. As a final touch, she fastened about her head a piece of blue ribbon, the band of cheap silk making the flash in her black eyes the brighter.

Sally left the house and started across the rubbish-littered yard. A short distance from the cabin she stopped to look about her.

"I'm dog-tired of it all," she said fiercely. "I hates the house. I hates the whole place, an' more'n all I hates Jim."

She turned, scowling, and walked between the rows of growing corn that reached to the edge of the clearing. Here began the pinewoods, the one saving touch nature has given to this land. Beneath the grateful shade she hastened her steps. The trees stood in endless disordered ranks, rising straight and bare of branch until high aloft their spreading tops caught the sunlight.

A quarter of a mile brought her to the lowland. She went down the slight decline and stepped within the cane-brake. Here gloom closed about her. The thickly growing cane reached to twice her height. Above the cane the cypress spread its branches, draped with the sad gray moss of the South. No sun's ray struggled through the rank foliage to lighten the sodden earth beneath. Sally picked her way slowly through the swamp, peering cautiously beyond each fallen log before venturing a further step. Crawfish scuttled backward from her path to slip down the mud chimneys of their homes. The black earth and decaying plants filled the hot, still air with noisome odors. Thousands of hidden insects sounded through the dank stretches their grating calls. Slimy water oozed from beneath the heavy soles of her brogans, green and purple bubbles were left in each footprint, bubbles with iridescent oily skins.

As she went around a sharp turn she was caught up and lifted clear from the ground in the arms of a young man—a boy of twenty or therabout.

"Oh, Bob, you scairt me—you certainly air rough!" Without words he kissed her again and again.

"Now, Bob, you quit! Ain't you had enough?"

"Could I ever have enough? Oh, Sally, I love you so!" The words trembled from the boy.

"You certainly ain't like none of 'em 'round hyar, Bob." There was some pride in Sally's drawling voice. "I never seed none of the men folks act with gals like you does."

"There's no other girl like you to make them." Then, holding her from him, he went on fiercely: "You don't let any of them try it, do you?"

Sally smiled up into his glowing eyes.

"You knows I don't. They'd be afeard of Jim."

The blood rushed to the boy's cheeks, his arms dropped to his side; he stood sobered.

"Sally, we can't go on this way any longer. That's why I asked you to come to the river to-day."

"What's a-goin' to stop us?" A frightened look crossed the woman's face.

"I'm going away."

She made a quick step toward him.

"You ain't lost your job on the new railroad?"

"No. Come down to the boat where we can talk this over."

He helped her down the bank of the creek to a flat-bottomed skiff, and seated her in the stern with a touch of courtesy before taking the cross seat facing her.

"No, I haven't lost my job," he began earnestly, "but my section of the road is about finished. They'll move me to another residency farther up the line in about a week."

She sat silent a moment, her black eyes wide with question. He searched them for some sign of sorrow.

"What kin I do after you air gone?"

There was a hopeless note in her voice; it pleased the boy.

"That's the point: instead of letting them move me, I'm going to move myself." He paused that she might get the full meaning of his coming words.

"I'm going away from here to-night, and I'm going to take you with me."

"No, no! I dasn't!" She shrank before his steady gaze.

He moved swiftly across to her. Throwing his arms around her, he poured out his words.

"Yes! You will! You must! You love me, don't you?"

Sally nodded in helpless assent.

"Better than anything in this world?"

Again Sally nodded.

"Then listen. To-night at twelve you come to the river. I'll be waiting for you at the edge of the swamp. We'll row down to Brewton. We can easily catch the six-twenty to Mobile, and, once there, we'll begin to live," he finished grandly.

"But I can't! Air you crazy? How kin I git away an' Jim right in the house?"

"I've thought of all that; you just let him see this." He drew a bottle from beneath the seat. "You know what he'll do to this; it's the strongest corn whisky I could find."

"Oh, Bob! I'm a-scairt to."

"Don't you love me?" His young eyes looked reproach.

Sally threw both arms about the boy's neck and drew his head down to her lips. Then she pushed him from her.

"Bob, is it so what the men-folks all say, that the railroad gives you a hundred dollars every month?"

He laughed. "Yes, you dear girl, and more. I get a hundred and a quarter, and I've been getting it for two years in this God-forsaken country, and nothing to spend it on. I've got over a thousand dollars saved up."

The woman's eyes widened. She kissed the boy on the mouth.

"They 'lows as how you're the smartest engineer on the road."

The boy's head was held high.

Sally made some mental calculations before she spoke again.

"Oh, Bob, I jes' cain't. I'm a-scairt to."

He caught her to him. A man of longer experience might have noted the sham in her reluctance.

"My darling, what are you afraid of?" he cried.

"What air we a-goin' to do after we gits to Mobile?"

"Oh, I've thought of everything. They're building a new line down in Texas. We'll go there. I'll get another job as resident engineer. I have my profession," he ended proudly.

"You might git tired, and want to git shed of me Bob."

He smothered her words under fierce kisses. His young heart beat at bursting pressure. In bright colours he pictured the glory of Mobile, New Orleans, and all the world that lay before them to love each other in.

When Sally left the boat she had promised to come. Where the pine-trees meet the cane-brake he would be waiting for her, at midnight.

At the top of the bank she turned to wave.

"Wait! Wait!" called the boy. He rushed up the slope.

"Quit, Bob, you're hurtin' me." She tore herself from his arms and hastened back along the slimy path. When she reached the pinewood she paused.

"More'n a thousand dollars!" she murmured, and a slow, satisfied smile crossed her shrewd face.

The sun, now directly over the tops of the trees, shot its scorching rays through the foliage. They struck the earth in vertical shafts, heating it to the burning point. Not a breath stirred the glistening pine-needles on the towering branches. It was one of those noon-times which, in the moisture-charged air of southern Alabama, makes life a steaming hell to all living things save reptiles and lovers.

Reaching the cabin, Sally went first to the kitchen room. She opened a cupboard and, taking the cork from the bottle, placed the whisky on the top shelf and closed the wooden door.

She crossed the dog-trot to the sleeping-room; a spitting snarl greeted her entrance. In the center of the bed crouched the yellow cat, its eyes gleaming, every muscle over its bony frame drawn taut, ready for the spring. The woman, startled, drew back. The cat moved on stiff legs nearer. Unflinchingly they glared into each other's eyes.

"Git out of hyar afore I kill yer! You yaller devil!" Sally's voice rang hard as steel.

The cat stood poised at the edge of the bed, its glistening teeth showing in its wide mouth. Without an instant's shift of her defiant stare, Sally wrenched a shoe from her foot. The animal with spread claws sprang straight for the woman's throat. The cat and the heavy brogan crashed together in mid-air. Together they fell to the floor; the cat landed lightly, silently, and bounded through the open door.

Sally fell back against the log wall of the cabin, feeling the skin at her throat with trembling fingers. . . .

"Jim! Oh-h, Jim!" Sally called from the cabin. "Come on in, yer supper's ready."

"He ain't took nothin' to drink to-day," she thought. "It's nigh three months now, he'll be 'most crazy."

The man took a few sticks of wood from the ground, and came on dragging feet through the gloom. As Sally watched his listless approach she felt in full force the oppressive melancholy of her dismal surroundings. Awakened by the boy's enthusiastic plans, imagination stirred within her. In the distance a girdled pine stood clear-cut against the horizon. Its bark peeled and fallen left the dead, naked trunk the color of dried bones. Near the stunted top one bare limb stretched out. Unnoticed a thousand times before, to the woman it looked tonight a ghostly gibbet against the black sky.

Sally shuddered and went into the lighted kitchen.

"I jes' kilt a rattler down by the wood-pile." Jim threw down his load and drew a splint-bottomed chair to the table.

"Ground-rattler, Jim?"

"Naw, sir-ee! A hell-bendin' big diamondback."

"Did you hurt the skin?" Sally asked quickly.

"Naw. I chopped his neck clean, short to the haid. An' I done it so durn quick his fangs is a-stickin' out yit, I reckon."

"Did he strike at you?"

"Yes, sir-ee, an' the pizen came out of his mouth jes' like a fog."

"Ah, you're foolin' me!"

"No, I ain't neither. I've heard tell of it, bit I never seed it afore. The ground was kinda black whar he lit, an' jes' as I brought the axe down on him, thar I seed a little puff like, same as white steam, in front of his mouth."

"How big was he, Jim?"

"'Leven rattle an' a button."

"Did you skin him?"

"Naw, it was too durn dark, but I hung him high up, so's the hawgs won't git at him. His skin 'll fotch of' bits down at Andalushy."

"Ax 'em six, Jim, them big ones gittin' kinda skeerce."

Jim finished his supper in silence; the killing of the snake had provided more conversation than was usual during three meals among pinewoods people.

As Sally was clearing away the dishes, the yellow cat came through the door. Slinking close to the wall, it avoided the woman, and sprang upon the knees of its master. Jim grinned into the eyes of the beast and began stroking its coarse hair. The cat set up a grating purr.

Sally looked at the two for a moment in silence.

"Jim, you gotta kill that cat."

Jim's grin widened, showing his tobacco-stained teeth.

"Jim, I'm a-tellin' you, you gotta kill that cat."

"An' I'm a-tellin' you I won't."

"Jim, it sprung at me to-day, an' would have hurt me somethin' turrible if I hadn't hit it over the haid with my shoe."

"Well, you must 'a' done somethin' to make him. You leave him alone an' he won't pester you."

The woman hesitated; she looked at the man as yet undecided; after a moment she spoke again.

"Jim Gantt, I'm axin' you for the las' time, which does you think more'n of, me or that snarlin' varmint?"

"He don't snarl at me so much as you does," the man answered doggedly. "Anyway, I ain't a-goin' to kill him; an' you gotta leave him alone, too. You jes' min yer own business an' go tote the mattress out on the trot. It's too durn hot to sleep in the house."

The woman passed behind him to the cupboard, reached up, opened wide the wooden door, and went out of the room.

Jim stroked the cat, its grating purr growing louder in the stillness.

A minute passed.

Into the dull eyes of the man a glitter came, and grew. Slowly he lifted his head. Farther and farther his chin drew up until the cords beneath the red skin of his neck stood out in ridges. The nostrils of his bony nose quivered, he sniffed the hot air like a dog straining to catch a distant scent. His tongue protruded and moved from side to side across his lips.

Standing in the darkness without, the woman smiled grimly.

Abruptly the man rose. The forgotten cat fell, twisted in the air, and lighted on its feet. Jim wheeled and strode to the cupboard. As his hand closed about the bottle, the gleam in his eyes became burning flames. He jerked the bottle from the shelf, threw his head far back. The fiery liquor ran down his throat. He returned to his seat; the cat rubbed its ribbed flank against his leg, he stooped and lifted it to the table. Waving the bottle in front of the yellow beast he laughed:

"Here's to yer—an' to'ad yer!" and swallowed half a tumblerful of the colorless liquid.

Sally dragged the shuck mattress to the dog-trot. Fully dressed, she lay waiting for midnight.

An hour went by before Jim shivered the empty bottle against the log wall of the kitchen. Pressing both hands hard upon the table, he heaved himself to his feet, upsetting the candle in the effort. He leered at the flame and slapped his bare palm down on it. The hot, melted wax oozed up, unheeded, between his fingers. Clinging to the tabletop, he turned himself toward the open door, steadied his swaying body for an instant, then lurched forward. His shoulder crashed against the doorpost, his body spun halfway round. The man fell flat upon his back, missing the mattress by a yard. The back of his head struck hard on the rough boards of the porch floor. He lay motionless, his feet sticking straight up on the doorsill.

The yellow cat sprang lightly over the fallen body and went out into the night . . .

Wide-eyed, the woman lay, watching. After moments of tense listening the sound of faint breathing came to her from the prone figure. Sally frowned. "He's too no 'count to git kilt," she said aloud, and turned on her side. She judged, from the stars, it was not yet eleven. Drowsiness came; she fell into uneasy slumber.

Out in the night the yellow cat was prowling. It stopped near the wood-pine. With extended paw, it touched lightly something that lay on the ground. Its long teeth fastened upon it. The cat slunk off toward the house. Without sound it sprang to the floor of the dog-trot. Stealthily, its body crouched low, it started to cross through the open way. As it passed the woman she muttered and struck out in her sleep. The cat flattened to the floor. Near the moving arm, the thing it carried fell from its teeth. The beast scurried out across the opening.

The night marched on to the sound of a million voices calling shrilly through the gloom.

The woman awoke. The stars glowed pale from a cloudy midnight sky. She reached out her right hand, palm down, to raise herself from the bed, throwing her full weight upon it. Two needlepoints pierced her wrist. A smothered cry was wrung from her lips. She reached with her left hand to pluck at the hurt place. It touched something cold, something hard and clammy, some dead thing. She jerked back the hand. A scream shivered through the still air. Pains becoming instantly acute, unbearable, darted through her arm. Again she tried to pull away the torturing needle points. Her quivering hand groped aimlessly in the darkness. She could not force herself, a second time, to touch the dead, clinging thing at her wrist. Screaming, she dragged herself to the man.

"Jim, I'm hurt, help me! Help me!"

The man did not move.

"Jim, wake up! Help me!" she wailed uselessly to the inert man.

The terrifying pain spurted from wrist to shoulder. With her clenched left hand she beat against the man's upturned face.

"You drunken fool, help me! Take this thing away!"

The man lay torpid beneath her pounding fist . . .

Along the path to Pigeon Creek, where the pinewoods run into the cane-brake, a boy waited; waited until the eastern sky grew from black to gray. Then with cautious tread he began to move, his face turned toward the cabin. As he neared the clearing the gray in the east changed to red. He left the woods and entered the field of corn. His footfalls made no sound on the earth between the furrows.

At the cabin he drew close against the wall and listened. A man's heavy breathing reached his straining ears. Slowly he moved toward the opening in the middle of the house. Above the breathing he heard a grating noise; between the deep-drawn breaths and the grating, another sound came to him; a harsh, rhythmic scratching.

The edge of the sun rose abruptly above the flat earth, sending light within the opening.

The boy thrust his head around the angle. A yellow cat was sitting at the foot of the mattress. From its throat grating purrs came in regular measure; between each purr the beast's spread claws clutched and released the stiff ticking.

Beyond lay the man.

Between the cat and the man, stretched across the shuck bed, was the woman; her glassy eyes staring up into the grinning face of the cat. From her shoulder, reaching out toward the boy, was a livid, turgid thing; a hand and arm, puffed beyond all human shape. From the swollen wrist, its poisoned fangs sunk deep into an artery, hung the mangled head of a snake.

The swaying corn blades whipped against the boy's white face as he fled between the rows.

The Brazilian Cat

[ARTHUR CONAN DOYLE]

It is hard luck on a young fellow to have expensive tastes, great expectations, aristocratic connections, but no actual money in his pocket, and no profession by which he may earn any. The fact was that my father, a good, sanguine, easygoing man, had such confidence in the wealth and benevolence of his bachelor elder brother, Lord Southerton, that he took it for granted that I, his only son, would never be called upon to earn a living for myself. He imagined that if there were not a vacancy for me on the great Southerton Estates, at least there would be found some post in that diplomatic service which still remains the special preserve of our privileged classes. He died too early to realize how false his calculations had been. Neither my uncle nor the State took the slightest notice of me, or showed any interest in my career. An occasional brace of pheasants, or basket of hares, was all that ever reached me to remind me that I was heir to Otwell House and one of the richest estates in the country. In the meantime, I found myself a bachelor and man about town, living in a suite of apartments in Grosvenor Mansions, with no occupation save that of pigeon shooting and polo playing at Hurlingham. Month by month I realized that it was more and more difficult to get the brokers to renew my bills, or to cash any further post-obits upon an unentailed property. Ruin lay right across my path, and every day I saw it clearer, nearer, and more absolutely unavoidable.

What made me feel my own poverty the more was that, apart from the great wealth of Lord Southerton, all my other relations were fairly well-to-do. The nearest of these was Everard King, my father's nephew and my own first cousin, who had spent an adventurous life in Brazil, and had now returned to this country to settle down on his fortune. We never knew how he made his money, but he appeared to have plenty of it, for he bought the estate of Grey-lands, near Clipton-on-the-Marsh, in Suffolk. For the first year of his residence in England he took no more notice of me than my miserly uncle; but at last one summer morning, to my very great relief and joy, I received a letter asking me to come down that very day and spend a short visit at Greylands Court. I was expecting a rather long visit to Bankruptcy Court at the time, and this interruption seemed almost providential. If I could only get on terms with this unknown relative of mine, I might pull through yet. For the family credit he could not let me go entirely to the wall. I ordered my valet to pack my valise, and I set off the same evening for Clipton-on-the-Marsh.

After changing at Ipswich, a little local train deposited me at a small, deserted station lying amidst a rolling grassy country, with a sluggish and winding river curving in and out amidst the valleys, between high, silted banks, which showed that we were within reach of the tide. No carriage was awaiting me (I found afterwards that my telegram had been delayed), so I hired a dogcart at the local inn. The driver, an excellent fellow, was full of my relative's praises, and I learned from him that Mr. Everard King was already a name to conjure with in that part of the county. He had entertained the schoolchildren, he had thrown his grounds open to visitors, he had subscribed to charities—in short, his benevolence had been so universal that my driver could only account for it on the supposition that he had parliamentary ambitions.

My attention was drawn away from my driver's panegyric by the appearance of a very beautiful bird which settled on a telegraph-post beside the road. At first I thought that it was a jay, but it was larger, with a brighter plumage. The driver accounted for its presence at once by saying that it belonged to the very man whom we were about to visit. It seems that the acclimatization of foreign creatures was one of his hobbies, and that he had brought with him from Brazil a number of birds and beasts which he was endeavoring to rear in England. When once we had passed the gates of Greylands Park we had ample evidence of this taste of his. Some small spotted deer, a curious wild pig known, I believe, as a peccary, a gorgeously feathered oriole, some sort of armadillo, and a singular lumbering in-toed beast like a very fat badger, were among the creatures which I observed as we drove along the winding avenue.

Mr. Everard King, my unknown cousin, was standing in person upon the steps of his house, for he had seen us in the distance, and guessed that it was I. His appearance was very homely and benevolent, short and stout, forty-five years old, perhaps, with a round, good-humored face, burned brown with the tropical sun, and shot with a thousand wrinkles. He wore white linen clothes, in true planter style, with a cigar between his lips, and a large Panama hat upon the back of his head. It was such a figure as one associates with a verandahed bungalow, and it looked curiously out of place in front of this broad, stone English mansion, with its solid wings and its Palladio pillars before the doorway.

"My dear!" he cried, glancing over his shoulder; "My dear, here is our guest! Welcome, welcome to Greylands! I am delighted to make your acquaintance, Cousin Marshall, and I take it as a great compliment that you should honor this sleepy little country place with your presence."

Nothing could be more hearty than his manner, and he set me at my ease in an instant. But it needed all his cordiality to atone for the frigidity and even rudeness of his wife, a tall, haggard woman, who came forward at his summons. She was, I believe, of Brazilian extraction, though she spoke excellent English, and I excused her manners on the score of her ignorance of our customs. She did not attempt to conceal, however, either then or afterwards, that I was no very welcome visitor at Greylands Court. Her actual words were, as a rule, courteous, but she was the possessor of a pair of particularly expressive dark eyes, and I read in them very clearly from the first that she heartily wished me back in London once more.

However, my debts were too pressing and my designs upon my wealthy relative were too vital for me to allow them to be upset by the ill-temper of his wife, so I disregarded her coldness and reciprocated the extreme cordiality of his welcome. No pains had been spared by him to make me comfortable. My room was a charming one. He implored me to tell him anything which could add to my happiness. It was on the tip of my tongue to inform him that a blank cheque would materially help towards that end, but I felt that it might be premature in the present state of our acquaintance. The dinner was excellent, and as we sat together afterwards over his Havanas and coffee, which later he told me was specially prepared upon his own plantation, it seemed to me that all my driver's eulogies were justified, and that I had never met a more large-hearted and hospitable man.

But, in spite of his cheery good nature, he was a man with a strong will and a fiery temper of his own. Of this I had an example upon the following morning. The curious aversion which Mrs. Everard King had conceived towards me was so strong, that her manner at breakfast was almost offensive. But her meaning became unmistakable when her husband had quitted the room.

"The best train in the day is at twelve-fifteen," said she.

"But I was not thinking of going today," I answered, frankly—perhaps even defiantly, for I was determined not to be driven out by this woman.

"Oh, if it rests with you—" said she, and stopped with a most insolent expression in her eyes.

"I am sure," I answered, "that Mr. Everard King would tell me if I were outstaying my welcome."

"What's this? What's this?" said a voice, and there he was in the room. He had overheard my last words, and a glance at our faces had told him the rest. In an instant his chubby, cheery face set into an expression of absolute ferocity.

"Might I trouble you to walk outside, Marshall?" said he. (I may mention that my own name is Marshall King.)

He closed the door behind me, and then, for an instant, I heard him talking in a low voice of concentrated passion to his wife. This gross breach of hospitality had evidently hit upon his tenderest point. I am no eavesdropper, so I walked out on to the lawn. Presently I heard a hurried step behind me, and there was the lady, her face pale with excitement, and her eyes red with tears.

"My husband has asked me to apologize to you, Mr. Marshall King," said she, standing with downcast eyes before me.

"Please do not say another word, Mrs. King."

Her dark eyes suddenly blazed out at me. "You fool!" she hissed, with frantic vehemence, and turning on her heel swept back to the house.

The insult was so outrageous, so insufferable, that I could only stand staring after her in bewilderment. I was still there when my host joined me. He was his cheery, chubby self once more.

"I hope that my wife has apologized for her foolish remarks," said he.

"Oh, yes—yes, certainly!"

He put his hand through my arm and walked with me up and down the lawn.

"You must not take it seriously," said he. "It would grieve me inexpressibly if you curtailed your visit by one hour. The fact is—there is no reason why there should be any concealment between relatives—that my poor dear wife is incredibly jealous. She hates that anyone—male or female—should for an instant come between us. Her ideal is a desert island and an eternal tête-à-tête. That gives you the clue to her actions, which are, I confess, upon this particular point, not very far removed from mania. Tell me that you will think no more of it."

"No, no; certainly not."

"Then light this cigar and come round with me and see my little menagerie."

The whole afternoon was occupied by this inspection, which included all the birds, beasts, and even reptiles which he had imported. Some were free, some in cages, a few actually in the house. He spoke with enthusiasm of his successes and his failures, his births and his deaths, and he would cry out in his delight, like a schoolboy, when, as we walked, some gaudy bird would flutter up from the grass, or some curious beast slink into the cover. Finally he led me down a corridor which extended from one wing of the house. At the end of this there was a heavy door with a sliding shutter in it, and beside it there projected from the wall an iron handle attached to a wheel and a drum. A line of stout bars extended across the passage.

"I am about to show you the jewel of my collection," said he. "There is only one other specimen in Europe, now that the Rotterdam cub is dead. It is a Brazilian cat."

"But how does that differ from any other cat?"

"You will soon see that," said he, laughing. "Will you kindly draw that shutter and look through?"

I did so, and found that I was gazing into a large, empty room, with stone flags, and small, barred windows upon the farther wall. In the centre of this room, lying in the middle of a golden patch of sunlight, there was stretched a huge creature, as large as a tiger, but as black and sleek as ebony. It was simply a very enormous and very well-kept black cat, and it cuddled up and basked in that yellow pool of light exactly as a cat would do. It was so graceful, so sinewy, and so gently and smoothly diabolical, that I could not take my eyes from the opening.

"Isn't he splendid?" said my host, enthusiastically.

"Glorious! I never saw such a noble creature."

"Some people call it a black puma, but really it is not a puma at all. That fellow is nearly eleven feet from tail to tip. Four years ago he was a little ball of back fluff, with two yellow eyes staring out of it. He was sold to me as a newborn cub up in the wild country at the head-waters of the Rio Negro. They speared his mother to death after she had killed a dozen of them."

"They are ferocious, then?"

"The most absolutely treacherous and blood-thirsty creatures upon earth. You talk about a Brazilian cat to an up-country Indian, and see him get the jumps. They prefer humans to game. This fellow has never tasted living blood yet, but when he does he will be a terror. At present he won't stand anyone but me in his den. Even Baldwin, the groom, dare not go near him. As to me, I am his mother and father in one."

As he spoke he suddenly, to my astonishment, opened the door and slipped in, closing it instantly behind him. At the sound of his voice the huge, lithe creature rose, yawned and rubbed its round, black head affectionately against his side, while he patted and fondled it.

"Now, Tommy, into your cage!" said he.

The monstrous cat walked over to one side of the room and coiled itself up under a grating. Everard King came out, and taking the iron handle which I have mentioned, he began to turn it. As he did so the line of bars in the corridor began to pass through a slot in the wall and closed up the front of this grating, so as to make an effective cage. When it was in position he opened the door once more and invited me into the room, which was heavy with the pungent, musty smell peculiar to the great carnivora.

"That's how we work it," said he. "We give him the run of the room for exercise, and then at night we put him in his cage. You can let him out by turning the handle from the passage, or you can, as you have seen, coop him up in the same way. No, no, you should not do that!"

I had put my hand between the bars to pat the glossy, heaving flank. He pulled it back, with a serious face.

"I assure you that he is not safe. Don't imagine that because I can take liberties with him anyone else can. He is very exclusive in his friends—aren't you, Tommy? Ah, he hears his lunch coming to him! Don't you, boy?"

A step sounded in the stone-flagged passage, and the creature had sprung to his feet, and was pacing up and down the narrow cage, his yellow eyes gleaming, and his scarlet tongue rippling and quivering over the white line of his jagged teeth. A groom entered with a coarse joint upon a tray, and thrust it through the bars to him. He pounced lightly upon it, carried it off to the corner, and there, holding it between his paws, tore and wrenched at it, raising his bloody muzzle every now and then to look at us. It was a malignant and yet fascinating sight.

"You can't wonder that I am fond of him, can you?" said my host, as we left the room, "especially when you consider that I have had the rearing of him. It was no joke bringing him over from the centre of South America; but here he is safe and sound—and, as I have said, far the most perfect specimen in Europe. The people at the Zoo are dying to have him, but I really can't part with him. Now, I think that I have inflicted my hobby upon you long enough, so we cannot do better than follow Tommy's example, and go to our lunch."

My South American relative was so engrossed by his grounds and their curious occupants, that I hardly gave him credit at first for having any interests outside them. That he had some, and pressing ones, was soon borne in upon me by the number of telegrams which he received. They arrived at all hours, and were always opened by him with the utmost eagerness and anxiety upon his face. Sometimes I imagined that it must be the Turf, and sometimes the Stock Exchange, but certainly he had some very urgent business going forwards which was not transacted upon the Downs of Suffolk. During the six days of my visit he had never fewer than three or four telegrams a day, and sometimes as many as seven or eight.

I had occupied these six days so well, that by the end of them I had succeeded in getting upon the most cordial terms with my cousin. Every night we had sat up late in the billiard-room, he telling me the most extraordinary stories of his adventures in America—stories so desperate and reckless, that I could hardly associate them with the brown little, chubby man before me. In return, I ventured upon some of my own reminiscences of London life, which interested him so much, that he vowed he would come up to Grosvenor Mansions and stay with me. He was anxious to see the faster side of city life, and certainly, though I say it, he could not have chosen a more competent guide. It was not until the last day of my visit that I ventured to approach that which was on my mind. I told him frankly about my pecuniary difficulties and my impending ruin, and I asked his advice—though I hoped for something more solid. He listened attentively, puffing hard at his cigar.

"But surely," said he, "you are the heir of our relative, Lord Southerton?"

"I have every reason to believe so, but he would never make me any allowance."

"No, no, I have heard of his miserly ways. My poor Marshall, your position has been a very hard one. By the way, have you heard any news of Lord Southerton's health lately?"

"He has always been in a critical condition ever since my childhood."

"Exactly—a creaking hinge, if ever there was one. Your inheritance may be a long way off. Dear me, how awkwardly situated you are!"

"I had some hopes, sir, that you, knowing all the facts, might be inclined to advance—"

"Don't say another word, my dear boy," he cried, with the utmost cordiality; "we shall talk it over tonight, and I give you my word that whatever is in my power shall be done."

I was not sorry that my visit was drawing to a close, for it is unpleasant to feel that there is one person in the house who eagerly desires your departure. Mrs. King's sallow face and forbidding eyes had become more and more hateful to me. She was no longer actively rude—her fear of her husband prevented her—but she pushed her insane jealousy to the extent of ignoring me, never addressing me, and in every way making my stay at Greylands as uncomfortable as she could. So offensive was her manner during that last day, that I should certainly have left had it not been for that interview with my host in the evening which would, I hoped, retrieve my broken fortunes.

It was very late when it occurred, for my relative, who had been receiving even more telegrams than usual during the day, went off to his study after dinner, and only emerged when the household had retired to bed. I heard him go round locking the doors, as custom was of a night, and finally he joined me in the billiard-room. His stout figure was wrapped in a dressing-gown, and he wore a pair of red Turkish slippers without any heels. Settling down into an armchair, he brewed himself a glass of grog, in which I could not help noticing that the whisky considerably predominated over the water.

"My word!" said he, "what a night!"

It was, indeed. The wind was howling and screaming round the house, and the latticed windows rattled and shook as if they were coming in. The glow of the yellow lamps and the flavor of our cigars seemed the brighter and more fragrant for the contrast.

"Now, my boy," said my host, "we have the house and the night to ourselves. Let me have an idea of how your affairs stand, and I will see what can be done to set them in order. I wish to hear every detail."

Thus encouraged, I entered into a long exposition, in which all my tradesmen and creditors from my landlord to my valet, figured in turn. I had notes in my pocketbook, and I marshaled my facts, and gave, I flatter myself, a very businesslike statement of my own unbusinesslike ways and lamentable position. I was depressed, however, to notice that my companion's eyes were vacant and his attention elsewhere. When he did occasionally throw out a remark it was so entirely perfunctory and pointless, that I was sure he had not in the least followed my remarks. Every now and then he roused himself and put on some show of interest, asking me to repeat or to explain more fully, but it was always to sink once more into the same brown study. At last he rose and threw the end of his cigar into the grate.

"I'll tell you what, my boy," said he. "I never had a head for figures, so you will excuse me. You must jot it all down upon paper, and let me have a note of the amount. I'll understand it when I see it in black and white."

The proposal was encouraging. I promised to do so.

"And now it's time we were in bed. By Jove, there's one o'clock striking in the hall."

The tingling of the chiming clock broke through the deep roar of the gale. The wind was sweeping past with the rush of a great river.

"I must see my cat before I go to bed," said my host. "A high wind excites him. Will you come?"

"Certainly," said I.

"Then tread softly and don't speak, for everyone is asleep."

We passed quietly down the lamp-lit Persian-rugged hall, and through the door at the farther end. All was dark in the stone corridor, but a stable lantern hung on a hook, and my host took it down and lit it. There was no grating visible in the passage, so I knew that the beast was in its cage.

"Come in!" said my relative, and opened the door.

A deep growling as we entered showed that the storm had really excited the creature. In the flickering light of the lantern, we saw it, a huge black mass coiled in the corner of its den and throwing a squat, uncouth shadow upon the whitewashed wall. Its tail switched angrily among the straw.

"Poor Tommy is not in the best of tempers," said Everard King, holding up the lantern and looking in at him. "What a black devil he looks, doesn't he? I must give him a little supper to put him in a better humor. Would you mind holding the lantern for a moment?"

I took it from his hand and he stepped to the door.

"His larder is just outside here," said he. "You will excuse me for an instant won't you?" He passed out, and the door shut with a sharp metallic click behind him.

That hard crisp sound made my heart stand still. A sudden wave of terror passed over me. A vague perception of some monstrous treachery turned me cold. I sprang to the door, but there was no handle upon the inner side.

"Here!" I cried. "Let me out!"

"All right! Don't make a row!" said my host from the passage. "You've got the light all right."

"Yes, but I don't care about being locked in alone like this."

"Don't you?" I heard his hearty, chuckling laugh. "You won't be alone long."

"Let me out, sir!" I repeated angrily. "I tell you I don't allow practical jokes of this sort."

"Practical is the word," said he, with another hateful chuckle. And then suddenly I heard, amidst the roar of the storm, the creak and whine of the winch-handle turning and the rattle of the grating as it passed through the slot. Great God, he was letting loose the Brazilian cat!

In the light of the lantern I saw the bars sliding slowly before me. Already there was an opening a foot wide at the farther end. With a scream I seized the last bar with my hands and pulled with the strength of a madman. I was a madman with rage and horror. For a minute or more I held the thing motionless. I knew that he was straining with all his force upon the handle, and that the leverage was sure to overcome me. I gave inch by inch, my feet sliding along the stones, and all the time I begged and prayed this inhuman monster to save me from this horrible death. I conjured him by his kinship. I reminded him that I was his guest; I begged to know what harm I had ever done him. His only answers were the tugs and jerks upon the handle, each of which, in spite of all my struggles, pulled another bar through the opening. Clinging and clutching, I was dragged across the whole front of the cage, until at last, with aching wrists and lacerated fingers, I gave up the hopeless struggle. The grating clanged back as

I released it, and an instant later I heard the shuffle of the Turkish slippers in the passage, and the slam of the distant door. Then everything was silent.

The creature had never moved during this time. He lay still in the corner, and his tail had ceased switching. This apparition of a man adhering to his bars and dragged screaming across him had apparently filled him with amazement. I saw his great eyes staring steadily at me. I had dropped the lantern when I seized the bars, but it still burned upon the floor, and I made a movement to grasp it, with some idea that its light might protect me. But the instant I moved, the beast gave a deep and menacing growl. I stopped and stood still, quivering with fear in every limb. The cat (if one may call so fearful a creature by so homely a name) was not more than ten feet from me. The eyes glimmered like two disks of phosphorus in the darkness. They appalled and yet fascinated me. I could not take my own eyes from them. Nature plays strange tricks with us at such moments of intensity, and those glimmering lights waxed and waned with a steady rise and fall. Sometimes they seemed to be tiny points of extreme brilliancy—little electric sparks in the black obscurity—then they would widen and widen until all that corner of the room was filled with their shifting and sinister light. And then suddenly they went out altogether.

The beast had closed its eyes. I do not know whether there may be any truth in the old idea of the dominance of the human gaze, or whether the huge cat was simply drowsy, but the fact remains that, far from showing any symptom of attacking me, it simply rested its sleek, black head upon its huge forepaws and seemed to sleep. I stood, fearing to move lest I should rouse it into malignant life once more. But at least I was able to think clearly now that the baleful eyes were off me. Here I was shut up for the night with the ferocious beast. My own instincts, to say nothing of the words of the plausible villain who laid this trap for me, warned me that the animal was as savage as its master. How could I stave it off until morning? The door was hopeless, and so were the narrow, barred windows. There was no shelter anywhere in the bare, stone-flagged room. To cry for assistance was absurd. I knew that this den was an outhouse, and that the corridor which connected it with the house was at least a hundred feet long. Besides, with the gale thundering outside, my cries were not likely to be heard. I had only my own courage and my own wits to trust to.

And then, with a fresh wave of horror, my eyes fell upon the lantern. The candle had burned low, and was already beginning to gutter. In ten minutes it would be out. I had only ten minutes then in which to do something, for I felt that if I were once left in the dark with that fearful beast I should be incapable of action. The very thought of it paralyzed me. I cast my despairing eyes round this chamber of death, and they rested upon one spot which seemed to promise I will not say safety, but less immediate and imminent danger than the open floor.

I have said that the cage had a top as well as a front, and this top was left standing when the front was wound through the slot in the wall. It consisted of bars at a few inches' interval, with stout wire netting between, and it rested upon a strong stanchion at each end. It stood now as a great barred canopy over the crouching figure in the corner. The space between this iron shelf and the roof may have been from two or three feet. If I could only get up there, squeezed in between bars and ceiling, I should have only one vulnerable side. I should be safe from below, from behind, and from each side. Only on the open face of it could I be attacked. There, it is true, I had no protection whatever; but at least, I should be out of the brute's path when he began to pace about his den. He would have to come out of his way to reach me. It was now or never, for if once the light were out it would be impossible. With a gulp in my throat I sprang up, seized the iron edge of the top, and swung myself panting on to it. I writhed in face downwards, and found myself looking straight into the terrible eyes and yawning jaws of the cat. Its fetid breath came up into my face like the steam from some foul pot.

It appeared, however, to be rather curious than angry. With a sleek ripple of its long, black back it rose, stretched itself, and then rearing itself on its hind legs, with one forepaw against the wall, it raised the other, and drew its claws across the wire meshes beneath me. One sharp, white hook tore through my trousers—for I may mention that I was still in evening dress—and dug a furrow in my knee. It was not meant as an attack, but rather as an experiment, for upon my giving a sharp cry of pain he dropped down again, and springing lightly into the room, he began walking swiftly round it, looking up every now and again in my direction. For my part I shuffled backwards until I lay with my back against the wall, screwing myself into the smallest space possible. The farther I got the more difficult it was for him to attack me.

He seemed more excited now that he had begun to move about, and he ran swiftly and noiselessly round and round the den, passing continually underneath the iron couch upon which I lay. It was wonderful to see so great a bulk passing like a shadow, with hardly the softest thudding of velvety pads. The candle was burning low—so low that I could hardly see the creature. And then, with a last flare and splutter it went out altogether. I was alone with the cat in the dark!

It helps one to face a danger when one knows that one has done all that possibly can be done. There is nothing for it then but to quietly await the result. In this case, there was no chance of safety anywhere except the precise spot where I was. I stretched myself out, therefore, and lay silently, almost breathlessly, hoping that the beast might forget my presence if I did nothing to remind him. I reckoned that it must already be two o'clock. At four it would be full dawn. I had not more than two hours to wait for daylight.

Outside, the storm was still raging, and the rain lashed continually against the little windows. Inside, the poisonous and fetid air was overpowering. I could neither hear nor see the cat. I tried to think about other things—but only one had power enough to draw my mind from my terrible position. That was the contemplation of my cousin's villainy, his unparalleled hypocrisy, his malignant hatred of me. Beneath that cheerful face there lurked the spirit of a mediaeval assassin. And as I thought of it I saw more clearly how cunningly the thing had been arranged. He had apparently gone to bed with the others. No doubt he had his witness to prove it. Then, unknown to them, he had slipped down, had lured me into his den and abandoned me. His story would be so simple. He had left me to finish my cigar in the billiard-room. I had gone down on my own account to have a last look at the cat. I had entered the room without observing that the cage was opened, and I had been caught. How could such a crime be brought home to him? Suspicion, per-haps—but proof, never!

How slowly those dreadful two hours went by! Once I heard a low, rasping sound, which I took to be the creature licking its own fur. Several times those greenish eyes gleamed at me through the dark-ness, but never in a fixed stare, and my hopes grew stronger that my presence had been forgotten or ignored. At last the least faint glimmer of light came through the windows—I first dimly saw them as two grey squares upon the black wall, then grey turned to white, and I could see my terrible companion once more. And he, alas, could see me!

It was evident to me at once that he was in a much more dangerous and aggressive mood than when I had seen him last. The cold of the morning had irri-tated him, and he was hungry as well. With a contin-ual growl he paced swiftly up and down the side of the room which was farthest from my refuge, his whiskers bristling angrily, and his tail switching and lashing. As he turned at the corners his savage eyes always looked upwards at me with a dreadful menace. I knew then that he meant to kill me. Yet I found myself even at that moment admiring the sinuous

grace of the devilish thing, its long, undulating, rippling movements, the gloss of its beautiful flanks, the
vivid, palpitating scarlet of the glistening tongue
which hung from the jet-black muzzle. And all the
time that deep, threatening growl was rising and rising in an unbroken crescendo. I knew that the crisis
was at hand.

It was a miserable hour to meet such a death—so
cold, so comfortless, shivering in my light dress
clothes upon this gridiron of torment upon which I
was stretched. I tried to brace myself to it, to raise
my soul above it, and at the same time, with the
lucidity which comes to a perfectly desperate man, I
cast round for some possible means of escape. One
thing was clear to me. If that front of the cage was
only back in its position once more, I could find a
sure refuge behind it. Could I possibly pull it back? I
hardly dared to move for fear of bringing the creature upon me. Slowly, very slowly, I put my hand
forward until it grasped the edge of the front, the
final bar which protruded through the wall. To my
surprise it came quite easily to my jerk. Of course
the difficulty of drawing it out arose from the fact
that I was clinging to it. I pulled again, and three
inches of it came through. It ran apparently on
wheels. I pulled again . . . and then the cat sprang!

It was so quick, so sudden, that I never saw it happen. I simply heard the savage snarl, and in an instant

afterwards the blazing yellow eyes, the flattened black head with its red tongue and flashing teeth, were within reach of me. The impact of the creature shook the bars upon which I lay, until I thought (as far as I could think of anything at such a moment) that they were coming down. The cat swayed there for an instant, the head and front paws quite close to me, the hind paws clawing to find a grip upon the edge of the grating. I heard the claws rasping as they clung to the wire-netting, and the breath of the beast made me sick. But its bound had been miscalculated. It could not retain its position. Slowly, grinning with rage, and scratching madly at the bars, it swung backwards and dropped heavily upon the floor. With a growl it instantly faced round to me and crouched for another spring.

I knew that the next few moments would decide my fate. The creature had learned by experience. It would not miscalculate again. I must act promptly, fearlessly, if I were to have a chance for life. In an instant I had formed my plan. Pulling off my dress-coat, I threw it down over the head of the beast. At the same moment I dropped over the edge, seized the end of the front grating, and pulled it frantically out of the wall.

It came more easily than I could have expected. I rushed across the room, bearing it with me; but, as I rushed, the accident of my position put me upon the outer side. Had it been the other way, I might have come off scathless. As it was, there was a moment's pause as I stopped it and tried to pass in through the opening which I had left. That moment was enough to give time to the creature to toss off the coat with which I had blinded him and to spring upon me. I hurled myself through the gap and pulled the rails to behind me, but he seized my leg before I could entirely withdraw it. One stroke of that huge paw tore off my calf as a shaving of wood curls off before a plane. The next moment, bleeding and fainting, I was lying among the foul straw with a line of friendly bars between me and the creature which ramped so frantically against them.

Too wounded to move, and too faint to be conscious of fear, I could only lie, more dead than alive, and watch it. It pressed its broad, black chest against the bars and angled for me with its crooked paws as I have seen a kitten do before a mousetrap. It ripped my clothes, but, stretch as it would, it could not quite reach me. I have heard of the curious numbing effect produced by wounds from the great carnivora, and now I was destined to experience it, for I had lost all sense of personality, and was as interested in the cat's failure or success as if it were some game which I was watching. And then gradually my mind drifted away into strange vague dreams, always with that black face and red tongue coming back into them, and so I lost myself in the nirvana of delirium, the blessed relief of those who are too sorely tried.

Tracing the course of events afterwards, I conclude that I must have been insensible for about two hours. What roused me to consciousness once more was that sharp metallic click which had been the precursor of my terrible experience. It was the shooting back of the spring lock. Then, before my senses were clear enough to entirely apprehend what they saw, I was aware of the round, benevolent face of my cousin peering in through the open door. What he saw evidently amazed him. There was the cat crouching on the floor. I was stretched upon my back in my shirtsleeves within the cage, my trousers torn to ribbons and a great pool of blood all round me. I can see his amazed face now, with the morning sunlight upon it. He peered at me, and peered again. Then he closed the door behind him, and advanced to the cage to see if I were really dead.

I cannot undertake to say what happened. I was not in a fit state to witness or to chronicle such events. I can only say that I was suddenly conscious that his face was away from me—that he was looking towards the animal.

"Good old Tommy!" he cried. "Good old Tommy!"

Then he came near the bars, with his back still towards me.

"Down, you stupid beast!" he roared. "Down, sir! Don't you know your master?"

Suddenly even in my bemuddled brain a remembrance came of those words of his when he had said that the taste of blood would turn the cat into a fiend. My blood had done it, but he was to pay the price.

"Get away!" he screamed. "Get away, you devil! Baldwin! Baldwin! Oh, my God!"

And then I heard him fall, and rise, and fall again, with a sound like the ripping of sacking. His screams grew fainter until they were lost in the worrying snarl. And then, after I thought that he was dead, I saw, as in a nightmare, a blinded, tattered, blood-soaked figure running wildly round the room—and that was the last glimpse which I had of him before I fainted once again.

I was many months in my recovery—in fact, I cannot say that I have ever recovered, for to the end of my days I shall carry a stick as a sign of my night with the Brazilian cat. Baldwin, the groom, and the other servants could not tell what had occurred, when, drawn by the death-cries of their master, they found me behind the bars, and his remains—or what they afterwards discovered to be his remains—in the clutch of the creature which he had reared. They stalled him off with hot irons, and afterwards shot him through the loophole of the door before they could finally extricate me. I was carried to my bedroom, and there, under the roof of my would-be murderer, I remained between life and death for several weeks. They had sent for a surgeon from Clipton and a nurse from London, and in a month I was able to be carried to the station, and so conveyed back once more to Grosvenor Mansions.

I have one remembrance of that illness, which might have been part of the ever-changing panorama conjured up by a delirious brain were it not so definitely fixed in my memory. One night, when the nurse was absent, the door of my chamber opened, and a tall woman in blackest mourning slipped into the room. She came across to me, and as she bent her sallow face I saw by the faint gleam of the night-light that it was the Brazilian woman whom my cousin had married. She stared intently into my face, and her expression was more kindly than I had ever seen it.

"Are you conscious?" she asked.

I feebly nodded—for I was still very weak.

"Well; then, I only wished to say to you that you have yourself to blame. Did I not do all I could for you? From the beginning I tried to drive you from the house. By every means, short of betraying my husband, I tried to save you from him. I knew that he had a reason for bringing you here. I knew that he would never let you get away again. No one knew him as I knew him, who had suffered from him so often. I did not dare to tell you all this. He would have killed me. But I did my best for you. As things have turned out, you have been the best friend that I have ever had. You have set me free, and I fancied that nothing but death would do that. I am sorry if you are hurt, but I cannot reproach myself. I told you that you were a fool— and a fool you have been." She crept out of the room, the bitter, singular woman, and I was never destined to see her again. With what remained from her husband's property she went back to her native land, and I have heard that she afterwards took the veil at Pernambuco.

It was not until I had been back in London for some time that the doctors pronounced me to be well enough to do business. It was not a very welcome permission to me, for I feared that it would be the signal for an inrush of creditors; but it was Summers, my lawyer, who first took advantage of it.

"I am very glad to see that your lordship is so much better," said he. "I have been waiting a long time to offer my congratulations."

"What do you mean, Summers? This is no time for joking."

"I mean what I say," he answered. "You have been Lord Southerton for the last six weeks, but we feared that it would retard your recovery if you were to learn it."

Lord Southerton! One of the richest peers in England! I could not believe my ears. And then suddenly I thought of the time which had elapsed, and how it coincided with my injuries.

"Then Lord Southerton must have died about the same time that I was hurt?"

"His death occurred upon that very day." Summers looked hard at me as I spoke, and I am convinced—for he was a very shrewd fellow—that he had guessed the true state of the case. He paused for a moment as if awaiting a confidence from me, but I could not see what was to be gained by exposing such a family scandal.

"Yes, a very curious coincidence," he continued, with the same knowing look. "Of course, you are aware that your cousin Everard King was the next heir to the estates. Now, if it had been you instead of him who had been torn to pieces by this tiger, or whatever it was, then of course he would have been Lord Southerton at the present moment."

"No doubt," said I.

"And he took such an interest in it," said Summers. "I happen to know that the late Lord Southerton's valet was in his pay, and that he used to have telegrams from him every few hours to tell him how he was getting on. That would be about the time when you were down there. Was it not strange that he should wish to be so well informed, since he knew that he was not the direct heir?"

"Very strange," said I. "And now, Summers, if you will bring me my bills and a new cheque-book, we will begin to get things into order."

The White Cat

[W. W. JACOBS]

The traveler stood looking from the taproom window of the *Cauliflower* at the falling rain. The village street below was empty, and everything was quiet with the exception of the garrulous old man smoking with much enjoyment on the settle behind him.

"It'll do a power o' good," said the ancient, craning his neck round the edge of the settle and turning a bleared eye on the window. "I ain't like some folk; I never did mind a drop o' rain."

The traveler grunted and, returning to the settle opposite the old man, fell to lazily stroking a cat which had strolled, in attracted by the warmth of the small fire which smoldered in the grate.

"He's a good mouser," said the old man, "but I expect that Smith the landlord would sell 'im to anybody for arf a crown; but we 'ad a cat in Claybury once that you couldn't ha' bought for a hundred golden sovereigns."

The traveler continued to caress the cat.

"A white cat, with one yaller eye and one blue one," continued the old man. "It sounds queer, but it's as true as I sit 'ere wishing that I 'ad another mug o' ale as good as the last you gave me."

The traveler, with a start that upset the cat's nerves, finished his own mug, and then ordered both to be refilled. He stirred the fire into a blaze, and, lighting his pipe and putting one foot on to the hob, prepared to listen.

"It used to belong to old man Clark, young Joe Clark's uncle," said the ancient, smacking his lips delicately over the ale and extending a tremulous claw to the tobacco-pouch pushed towards him; "and he was never tired of showing it off to people. He used to call it 'is blue-eyed darling, and the fuss 'e made o' that cat was sinful.

"Young Joe Clark couldn't bear it, but being down in 'is uncle's will for five cottages and a bit o' land bringing in about forty pounds a year, he 'ad to 'ide his feelings and pretend as he loved it. He used to take it little drops o' cream and tit-bits o' meat, and old Clark was so pleased that 'e promised 'im that he should 'ave the cat along with all the other property when 'e was dead.

"Young Joe said he couldn't thank 'im enough, and the old man, who 'ad been ailing a long time, made 'im come up every day to teach 'im 'ow to take care of it arter he was gone. He taught Joe 'ow to cook its meat and then chop it up fine; 'ow it liked a clean saucer every time for its milk; and 'ow he wasn't to make a noise when it was asleep.

"'Take care your children don't worry it, Joe,' he ses one day, very sharp. 'One o' your boys was pulling its tail this morning, and I want you to clump his 'ead for 'im.'

"'Which one was it?' ses Joe.

"'The slobbery-nosed one,' ses old Clark.

"'I'll give 'im a clout as soon as I get 'ome,' ses Joe, who was very fond of 'is children.

"'Go and fetch 'im and do it 'ere,' ses the old man; 'that'll teach 'im to love animals.'

"Joe went off 'ome to fetch the boy, and arter his mother 'ad washed his face, and wiped his nose, an' put a clean pinneyfore on 'im, he took 'im to 'is uncle's and clouted his 'ead for 'im. Arter that Joe and 'is wife 'ad words all night long, and next morning old Clark, coming in from the garden, was just in time to see 'im kick the cat right acrost the kitchen.

"He could 'ardly speak for a minute, and when 'e could Joe see plain wot a fool he'd been. Fust of all 'e called Joe every name he could think of—which took 'im a long time—and then he ordered 'im out of 'is house.

"'You shall 'ave my money wen your betters have done with it,' he ses, 'and not afore. That's all you've done for yourself.'

"Joe Clark didn't know wot he meant at the time, but when old Clark died three months arterwards 'e found out. His uncle 'ad made a new will and left everything to old George Barstow for as long as the cat lived, providing that he took care of it. When the cat was dead the property was to go to Joe.

"The cat was only two years old at the time, and George Barstow, who was arf crazy with joy, said it shouldn't be 'is fault if it didn't live another twenty years.

"The funny thing was the quiet way Joe Clark took it. He didn't seem to be at all cut up about it, and when Henery Walker said it was a shame, 'e said he didn't mind, and that George Barstow was a old man, and he was quite welcome to 'ave the property as long as the cat lived.

"'It must come to me by the time I'm an old man,' he ses, 'ard that's all I care about.'

"Henery Walker went off, and as 'e passed the cottage where old Clark used to live, and which George Barstow 'ad moved into, 'e spoke to the old man over the palings and told 'im wot Joe Clark 'ad said.

George Barstow only grunted and went on stooping and prying over 'is front garden.

"'Bin and lost something?' ses Henery Walker, watching 'im.

"'No; I'm finding,' ses George Barstow, very fierce, and picking up something. 'That's the fifth bit o' powdered liver I've found in my garden this morning.'

"Henery Walker went off whistling, and the opinion he'd 'ad o' Joe Clark began to improve. He spoke to Joe about it that arternoon, and Joe said that if 'e ever accused 'im o' such a thing again he'd knock 'is 'ead off. He said that he 'oped the cat 'ud live to be a hundred, and that 'e'd no more think of giving it poisoned meat than Henery Walker would of paying for 'is drink so long as 'e could get anybody else to do it for 'im.

"They 'ad bets up at this 'ere *Cauliflower* public-'ouse that evening as to 'ow long that cat 'ud live. Nobody gave it more than a month, and Bill Chambers sat and thought o' so many ways o' killing it on the sly that it was wunnerful to hear 'im.

"George Barstow took fright when he 'eard of them, and the care 'e took o' that cat was wunnerful to behold. Arf its time it was shut up in the back bedroom, and the other arf George Barstow was fussing arter it till that cat got to hate 'im like pison.

Instead o' giving up work as he'd thought to do, 'e told Henery Walker that 'e'd never worked so 'ard in his life.

"'Wot about fresh air and exercise for it?' ses Henery.

"'Wot about Joe Clark?' ses George Barstow. 'I'm tied 'and and foot. I dursent leave the house for a moment. I ain't been to the *Cauliflower* since I've 'ad it, and three times I got out o' bed last night to see if it was safe.'

"'Mark my words,' ses Henery Walker; 'if that cat don't 'ave exercise, you'll lose it.'

"'I shall lose it if it does 'ave exercise,' ses George Barstow, 'that I know.'

"He sat down thinking arter Henery Walker 'ad gone, and then he 'ad a little collar and chain made for it, and took it out for a walk. Pretty nearly every dog in Claybury went with 'em, and the cat was in such a state o' mind afore they got 'ome he couldn't do anything with it. It 'ad a fit as soon as they got indoors, and George Barstow, who 'ad read about children's fits in the almanac, gave it a warm bath. It brought it round immediate, and then it began to tear round the room and up and downstairs till George Barstow was afraid to go near it.

"It was so bad that evening, sneezing, that George Barstow sent for Bill Chambers, who'd got a good name for doctoring animals, and asked 'im to give it something. Bill said he'd got some powders at 'ome that would cure it at once, and he went and fetched 'em and mixed one up with a bit o' butter.

"'That's the way to give a cat medicine,' he ses; 'smear it with the butter and then it'll lick it off, powder and all.'

"He was just going to rub it on the cat when George Barstow caught 'old of 'is arm and stopped 'im.

"'How do I know it ain't pison?' he ses. 'You're a friend o' Joe Clark's, and for all I know he may ha' paid you to pison it.'

"'I wouldn't do such a thing,' ses Bill. 'You ought to know me better than that.'

"'All right,' ses George Barstow; 'you eat it then, and I'll give you two shillings in stead o' one. You can easy mix some more.'

"'Not me,' ses Bill Chambers, making a face.

"'Well, three shillings, then,' ses George Barstow, getting more and more suspicious like; 'four shillings—five shillings.'

"Bill Chambers shook his 'ead, and George Barstow, more and more certain that he 'ad caught 'im trying to kill 'is cat and that 'e wouldn't eat the stuff, rose 'im up to ten shillings.

"Bill looked at the butter and then 'e looked at the ten shillings on the table, and at last he shut 'is eyes and gulped it down and put the money in 'is pocket.

"'You see, I 'ave to be careful, Bill,' ses George Barstow, rather upset.

"Bill Chambers didn't answer 'im. He sat there as white as a sheet, and making such extraordinary faces that George was arf afraid of 'im.

"'Anything wrong, Bill?' he ses at last.

"Bill sat staring at 'im, and then all of a sudden he clapped 'is 'andkerchief to 'is mouth and, getting up from his chair, opened the door and rushed out. George Barstow thought at fust that he 'ad eaten pison for the sake o' the ten shillings, but when 'e remembered that Bill Chambers 'ad got the most delikit stummick in Claybury he altered 'is mind.

"The cat was better next morning, but George Barstow had 'ad such a fright about it 'e wouldn't let it go out of 'is sight, and Joe Clark began to think that 'e would 'ave to wait longer for that property than 'e had thought, arter all. To 'ear 'im talk anybody'd ha' thought that 'e loved that cat. We didn't pay much attention to it up at the *Cauliflower* 'ere, except maybe to wink at 'im—a thing he couldn't a bear—but at 'ome, o' course, his young 'uns thought as everything he said was Gospel; and one day, coming 'ome from work, as he was passing George Barstow's he was paid out for his deceitfulness.

"'I've wronged you, Joe Clark,' ses George Barstow, coming to the door, 'and I'm sorry for it.'

"'Oh!' ses Joe, staring.

"'Give that to your little Jimmy,' ses George Barstow, giving 'im a shilling. 'I've give 'im one, but I thought arterwards it wasn't enough.'

"'What for?' ses Joe, staring at 'im agin.

"'For bringing my cat 'ome,' ses George Barstow. "''Ow it got out I can't think, but I lost it for three hours, and I'd about given it up when your little Jimmy brought it to me in 'is arms. He's a fine little chap and 'e does you credit.'

"Joe Clark tried to speak, but he couldn't get a word out, and Henery Walker, wot 'ad just come up and 'eard wot passed, took hold of 'is arm and helped 'im home. He walked like a man in a dream, but arf-way he stopped and cut a stick from the hedge to take 'ome to little Jimmy. He said the boy 'ad been asking him for a stick for some time, but up till then 'e'd always forgotten it.

"At the end o' the fust year that cat was still alive, to everybody's surprise; but George Barstow took such care of it 'e never let it out of 'is sight. Every time 'e went out he took it with 'im in a hamper, and, to prevent its being poisoned, he paid Isaac Sawyer, who 'ad the biggest family in Claybury, sixpence a week to let one of 'is boys taste its milk before it had it.

"The second year it was ill twice, but the horse-doctor that George Barstow got for it said that it was as 'ard as nails, and with care it might live to be twenty. He said that it wanted more fresh air and exercise; but when he 'eard 'ow George Barstow come by it he said that p'r'aps it would live longer indoors arter all.

"At last one day, when George Barstow 'ad been living on the fat o' the land for nearly three years, that cat got out agin. George 'ad raised the front-room winder two or three inches to throw something outside, and, afore he knew wot was 'appening, the cat was out-side and going up the road about twenty miles an hour.

"George Barstow went arter it, but he might as well ha' tried to catch the wind. The cat was arf wild with joy at getting out agin, and he couldn't get within arf a mile of it.

"He stayed out all day without food or drink, follering it about until it came on dark, and then, o' course, he lost sight of it, and, hoping against 'ope that it would come home for its food, he went 'ome and waited for it. He sat up all night dozing in a chair in the front room with the door left open, but it was all no use; and arter thinking for a long time wot was best to do, he went out and told some o' the folks it was lost and offered a reward of five pounds for it.

"You never saw such a hunt then in all your life. Nearly every man, woman, and child in Claybury left their work or school and went to try and earn that five pounds. By the arternoon George Barstow made it ten pounds provided the cat was brought 'ome safe and sound, and people as was too old to walk stood at their cottage doors to snap it up as it came by.

"Joe Clark was hunting for it 'igh and low, and so was 'is wife and the boys. In fact, I b'lieve that everybody in Claybury excepting the parson and Bob Pretty was trying to get that ten pounds.

"O' course, we could understand the parson—'is pride wouldn't let 'im; but a low, poaching, thieving rascal like Bob Pretty turning up 'is nose at ten pounds was more than we could make out. Even on the second day, when George Barstow made it ten pounds down and a shilling a week for a year besides, he didn't offer to stir; all he did was to try and make fun o' them as was looking for it.

"'Have you looked everywhere you can think of for it, Bill?' he ses to Bill Chambers. 'Yes, I 'ave,' ses Bill.

"'Well, then, you want to look everywhere else,' ses Bob Pretty. 'I know where I should look if I wanted to find it.'

"'Why don't you find it, then?' ses Bill.

"''Cos I don't want to make mischief,' ses Bob Pretty. 'I don't want to be unneighborly to Joe Clark by interfering at all.'

"'Not for all that money?' ses Bill.

"'Not for fifty pounds,' ses Bob Pretty; 'you ought to know me better than that, Bill Chambers.'

"'It's my belief that you know more about where that cat is than you ought to,' ses Joe Gubbins.

"'You go on looking for it, Joe,' ses Bob Pretty, grinning; 'it's good exercise for you, and you've only lost two days' work.'

"'I'll give you arf a crown if you let me search your 'ouse, Bob,' ses Bill Chambers, looking at 'im very 'ard.

"'I couldn't do it at the price, Bill,' ses Bob Pretty, shaking his 'ead. 'I'm a pore man, but I'm very partikler who I 'ave come into my 'ouse.'

"O' course, everybody left off looking at once when they heard about Bob—not that they believed that he'd be such a fool as to keep the cat in his 'ouse; and that evening, as soon as it was dark, Joe Clark went round to see 'im.

"'Don't tell me as that cat's found, Joe,' ses Bob Pretty, as Joe opened the door.

"'Not as I've 'eard of,' said Joe, stepping inside. 'I wanted to speak to you about it; the sooner it's found the better I shall be pleased.'

"'It does you credit, Joe Clark,' ses Bob Pretty.

"'It's my belief that it's dead,' ses Joe, looking at 'im very 'ard; 'but I want to make sure afore taking over the property.'

"Bob Pretty looked at 'im and then he gave a little cough. 'Oh, you want it to be found dead,' he ses.

"'Now, I wonder whether that cat's worth most dead or alive?'

"Joe Clark coughed then. 'Dead, I should think,' he ses at last. 'George Barstow's just 'ad bills printed offering fifteen pounds for it,' ses Bob Pretty.

"'I'll give that or more when I come into the property,' ses Joe Clark.

"'There's nothing like ready-money, though, is there?' ses Bob.

"'I'll promise it to you in writing, Bob,' ses Joe, trembling.

"'There's some things that don't look well in writing, Joe,' says Bob Pretty, considering; 'besides, why should you promise it to me?'

"'O' course, I meant if you found it,' ses Joe.

"'Well, I'll do my best, Joe,' ses Bob Pretty; 'and none of us can do no more than that, can they?'

"They sat talking and argufying over it for over an hour, and twice Bob Pretty got up and said 'e was going to see whether George Barstow wouldn't offer more. By the time they parted they was as thick as thieves, and next morning Bob Pretty was wearing Joe Clark's watch and chain, and Mrs. Pretty was up at Joe's 'ouse to see whether there was any of 'is furniture as she 'ad a fancy for.

"She didn't seem to be able to make up 'er mind at fust between a chest o' drawers that 'ad belonged to

Joe's mother and a grand-father clock. She walked from one to the other for about ten minutes, and then Bob, who 'ad come in to 'elp her, told 'er to 'ave both.

"'You're quite welcome,' he ses; 'ain't she, Joe?'

"Joe Clark said 'Yes,' and arter he 'ad helped them carry 'em 'ome the Prettys went back and took the best bedstead to pieces, cos Bob said as it was easier to carry that way. Mrs. Clark 'ad to go and sit down at the bottom o' the garden with the neck of 'er dress undone to give herself air, but when she saw the little Prettys each walking 'ome with one of 'er best chairs on their 'eads she got and walked up and down like a mad thing.

"'I'm sure I don't know where we are to put it all,' ses Bob Pretty to Joe Gubbins, wot was looking on with other folks, 'but Joe Clark is that generous he won't 'ear of our leaving anything.'

"'Has 'e gorn mad?' ses Bill Chambers, staring at 'im.

"'Not as I knows on,' ses Bob Pretty. 'It's 'is good-'artedness, that's all. He feels sure that that cat's dead, and that he'll 'ave George Barstow's cottage and furniture. I told 'im he'd better wait till he'd made sure, but 'e wouldn't.'

"Before they'd finished the Prettys 'ad picked that 'ouse as clean as a bone, and Joe Clark 'ad to go and get clean straw for his wife and children to sleep on; not that Mrs. Clark 'ad any sleep that night, nor Joe neither.

"Henery Walker was the fust to see what it really meant, and he went rushing off as fast as 'e could run to tell George Barstow. George couldn't believe 'im at fust, but when 'e did he swore that if a 'air of that cat's head was harmed 'e'd 'ave the law o' Bob Pretty, and arter Henery Walker 'ad gone 'e walked round to tell 'im so.

"'You're not yourself, George Barstow, else you wouldn't try and take away my character like that,' ses Bob Pretty.

"'Wot did Joe Clark give you all them things for?' ses George, pointing to the furniture.

"'Took a fancy to me, I s'pose,' ses Bob. 'People do sometimes. There's something about me at times that makes 'em like me.'

"'He gave 'em to you to kill my cat,' ses George Barstow. 'It's plain enough for any-body to see.'

"Bob Pretty smiled. 'I expect it'll turn up safe and sound one o' these days,' he ses, 'and then you'll come round and beg my pardon. P'r'aps—'

"'P'r'aps wot?' ses George Barstow, arter waiting a bit.

"'P'r'aps somebody 'as got it and is keeping it till you've drawed the fifteen pounds out o' the bank,' ses Bob, looking at 'im very hard.

"'I've taken it out o' the bank,' ses George, starting; 'if that cat's alive, Bob, and you've got it, there's the fifteen pounds the moment you 'and it over.'

"'Wot d'ye mean—me got it?' ses Bob Pretty. 'You be careful o' my character.'

'I mean if you know where it is,' ses George Barstow trembling all over.

"'I don't say I couldn't find it, if that's wot you mean,' ses Bob. 'I can gin'rally find things when I want to.'

"'You find me that cat, alive and well, and the money's yours, Bob,' ses George, 'ardly able to speak, now that 'e fancied the cat was still alive.

"Bob Pretty shook his 'ead. 'No; that won't do,' he ses. 'S'pose I did 'ave the luck to find that pore animal, you'd say I'd had it all the time and refuse to pay.'

"'I swear I wouldn't, Bob,' ses George Barstow, jumping up.

"'Best thing you can do if you want me to try and find that cat,' says Bob Pretty, 'is to give me the fifteen pounds now, and I'll go and look for it at once. I can't trust you, George Barstow.'

"'And I can't trust you,' ses George Barstow.

"'Very good,' ses Bob, getting up; 'there's no 'arm done. P'r'aps Joe Clark 'll find the cat is dead and p'r'aps you'll find it's alive. It's all one to me.'

"George Barstow walked off 'ome, but he was in such a state o' mind 'e didn't know wot to do. Bob Pretty turning up 'is nose at fifteen pounds like that made 'im think that Joe Clark 'ad promised to pay 'im more if the cat was dead; and at last, arter worrying about it for a couple o' hours, 'e came up to this 'ere *Cauliflower* and offered Bob the fifteen pounds.

"'Wot's this for?' ses Bob.

"'For finding my cat,' ses George.

"'Look here,' ses Bob, handing it back, 'I've 'ad enough o' your insults; I don't know where your cat is.'

"'I mean for trying to find it, Bob,' ses George Barstow.

"'Oh, well, I don't mind that,' ses Bob, taking it. 'I'm a 'ard-working man, and I've got to be paid for my time; it's on'y fair to my wife and children. I'll start now.'

"He finished up 'is beer, and while the other chaps was telling George Barstow wot a fool he was Joe Clark slipped out arter Bob Pretty and began to call 'im all the names he could think of.

"'Don't you worry,' ses Bob; 'the cat ain't found yet.'

"'Is it dead?' ses Joe Clark, 'ardly able to speak.

"''Ow should I know?' ses Bob; 'that's wot I've got to try and find out. That's wot you gave me your furniture for, and wot George Barstow gave me the fifteen pounds for, ain't it? Now, don't you stop me now, 'cos I'm goin' to begin looking.'

"He started looking there and then, and for the next two or three days George Barstow and Joe Clark see 'im walking up and down with his 'ands in 'is pockets looking over garden fences and calling 'Puss.' He asked everybody 'e see whether they 'ad seen a white cat with one blue eye and one yaller one, and every time 'e came into the *Cauliflower* he put his 'ead over the bar and called 'Puss,' 'cos, as 'e said, it was as likely to be there as anywhere else.

"It was about a week after the cat 'ad disappeared that George Barstow was standing at 'is door talking to Joe Clark, who was saying the cat must be dead and 'e wanted 'is property, when he sees a man coming up the road carrying a basket stop and speak to Bill Chambers. Just as 'e got near them an awful 'miaow' come from the basket and George Barstow and Joe Clark started as if they'd been shot.

"'He's found it?' shouts Bill Chambers, pointing to the man.

"'It's been living with me over at Ling for a week pretty nearly,' ses the man. 'I tried to drive it away several times, not knowing that there was fifteen pounds offered for it.'

"George Barstow tried to take 'old of the basket.

"'I want that fifteen pounds fust,' ses the man.

"'That's on'y right and fair, George,' ses Bob Pretty, who 'ad just come up. 'You've got all the luck, mate. We've been hunting 'igh and low for that cat for a week.'

"Then George Barstow tried to explain to the man and call Bob Pretty names at the same time; but it was all no good. The man said it 'ad nothing to do with 'im wot he 'ad paid to Bob Pretty; and at last they fetched Policeman White over from Cudford, and George Barstow signed a paper to pay five shillings a week till the reward was paid.

"George Barstow 'ad the cat for five years arter that, but he never let it get away agin. They got to like each other in time and died within a fortnight of each other, so that Joe Clark got 'is property arter all."

Who Was to Blame?

[ANTON CHEKHOV]

A s my uncle Pyotr Demyanitch, a lean, bilious collegiate councilor, exceedingly like a stale smoked fish with a stick through it, was getting ready to go to the high school, where he taught Latin, he noticed that the corner of his grammar was nibbled by mice.

"I say, Praskovya," he said, going into the kitchen and addressing the cook, "how is it we have got mice here? Upon my word! yesterday my top hat was nibbled, to-day they have disfigured my Latin grammar. . . . At this rate they will soon begin eating my clothes!"

"What can I do? I did not bring them in!" answered Praskovya.

"We must do something! You had better get a cat, hadn't you?"

"I've got a cat, but what good is it?"

And Praskovya pointed to the corner where a white kitten, thin as a match, lay curled up asleep beside a broom.

"Why is it no good?" asked Pyotr Demyanitch.

"It's young yet, and foolish. It's not two months old yet."

"H'm. . . . Then it must be trained. It had much better be learning instead of lying there."

Saying this, Pyotr Demyanitch sighed with a careworn air and went out of the kitchen. The kitten raised his head, looked lazily after him, and shut his eyes again.

The kitten lay awake thinking. Of what? Unacquainted with real life, having no store of accumulated impressions, his mental processes could only be instinctive, and he could but picture life in accordance with the conceptions that he had inherited, together with his flesh and blood, from his ancestors, the tigers (vide Darwin). His thoughts were of the nature of daydreams. His feline imagination pictured something like the Arabian desert, over which flitted shadows closely resembling Praskovya, the stove, the broom. In the midst of the shadows there suddenly appeared a saucer of milk; the saucer began to grow paws, it began moving and displayed a tendency to run; the kitten made a bound, and with a thrill of blood-thirsty sensuality thrust his claws into it.

When the saucer had vanished into obscurity a piece of meat appeared, dropped by Praskovya; the meat ran away with a cowardly squeak, but the kitten made a bound and got his claws into it. . . . Everything that rose before the imagination of the young dreamer had for its starting-point leaps, claws, and teeth. . . . The soul of another is darkness, and a cat's soul more than most, but how near the visions just described are to the truth may be seen from the following fact: under the influence of his day-dreams the kitten suddenly leaped up, looked with flashing eyes at Praskovya, ruffled up his coat, and making one bound, thrust his claws into the cook's skirt. Obviously he was born a mouse catcher, a worthy son of his bloodthirsty ancestors. Fate had destined him to be the terror of cellars, storerooms and corn-bins, and had it not been for education . . . we will not anticipate, however.

On his way home from the high school, Pyotr Demyanitch went into a general shop and bought a mousetrap for fifteen kopecks. At dinner he fixed a little bit of his rissole on the hook, and set the trap under the sofa, where there were heaps of the pupils' old exercise-books, which Praskovya used for various domestic purposes. At six o'clock in the evening, when the worthy Latin master was sitting at the table correcting his pupils' exercises, there was a sudden "*klop!*" so loud that my uncle started and dropped his pen. He went at once to the sofa and took out the trap. A neat little mouse, the size of a thimble, was sniffing the wires and trembling with fear.

"Aha," muttered Pyotr Demyanitch, and he looked at the mouse malignantly, as though he were about to give him a bad mark. "You are cau— aught, wretch! Wait a bit! I'll teach you to eat my grammar!"

Having gloated over his victim, Pyotr Demyanitch put the mouse-trap on the floor and called:

"Praskovya, there's a mouse caught! Bring the kitten here!"

"I'm coming," responded Praskovya, and a minute later she came in with the descendant of tigers in her arms.

"Capital!" said Pyotr Demyanitch, rubbing his hands. "We will give him a lesson. . . . Put him down opposite the mouse-trap . . . that's it. . . . Let him sniff it and look at it. . . . That's it. . . ."

The kitten looked wonderingly at my uncle, at his arm-chair, sniffed the mouse-trap in bewilderment, then, frightened probably by the glaring lamplight and the attention directed to him, made a dash and ran in terror to the door.

"Stop!" shouted my uncle, seizing him by the tail, "stop, you rascal! He's afraid of a mouse, the idiot! Look! It's a mouse! Look! Well? Look, I tell you!"

Pyotr Demyanitch took the kitten by the scruff of the neck and pushed him with his nose against the mouse-trap.

"Look, you carrion! Take him and hold him, Praskovya. . . . Hold him opposite the door of the trap. . . . When I let the mouse out, you let him go instantly. . . . Do you hear? . . . Instantly let go! Now!"

My uncle assumed a mysterious expression and lifted the door of the trap. . . . The mouse came out irresolutely, sniffed the air, and flew like an arrow under the sofa. . . . The kitten on being released darted under the table with his tail in the air.

"It has got away! got away!" cried Pyotr Demyanitch, looking ferocious. "Where is he, the scoundrel? Under the table? You wait . . ."

My uncle dragged the kitten from under the table and shook him in the air.

"Wretched little beast," he muttered, smacking him on the ear. "Take that, take that! Will you shirk it next time? Wr-r-r-etch . . ."

Next day Praskovya heard again the summons.

"Praskovya, there is a mouse caught! Bring the kitten here!"

After the outrage of the previous day the kitten had taken refuge under the stove and had not come out all night. When Praskovya pulled him out and, carrying him by the scruff of the neck into the study, set him down before the mousetrap, he trembled all over and mewed piteously.

"Come, let him feel at home first," Pyotr Demyanitch commanded. "Let him look and sniff. Look and learn! Stop, plague take you!" he shouted, noticing that the kitten was backing away from the mousetrap. "I'll thrash you! Hold him by the ear! That's it. . . . Well now, set him down before the trap . . ."

My uncle slowly lifted the door of the trap . . . the mouse whisked under the very nose of the kitten, flung itself against Praskovya's hand and fled under the cupboard; the kitten, feeling himself free, took a desperate bound and retreated under the sofa.

"He's let another mouse go!" bawled Pyotr Demyanitch. "Do you call that a cat? Nasty little beast! Thrash him! thrash him by the mousetrap!"

When the third mouse had been caught, the kitten shivered all over at the sight of the mousetrap and its inmate, and scratched Praskovya's hand. . . . After the fourth mouse my uncle flew into a rage, kicked the kitten, and said:

"Take the nasty thing away! Get rid of it! Chuck it away! It's no earthly use!"

A year passed, the thin, frail kitten had turned into a solid and sagacious tomcat. One day he was on his way by the back yards to an amatory interview. He had just reached his destination when he suddenly heard a rustle, and thereupon caught sight of a mouse which ran from a water-trough towards a stable; my hero's hair stood on end, he arched his back, hissed, and trembling all over, took to ignominious flight.

Alas! sometimes I feel myself in the ludicrous position of the flying cat. Like the kitten, I had in my day the honor of being taught Latin by my uncle. Now, whenever I chance to see some work of classical antiquity, instead of being moved to eager enthusiasm, I begin recalling, *ut consecutivum,* the irregular verbs, the sallow grey face of my uncle, the ablative absolute. . . . I turn pale, my hair stands up on my head, and, like the cat, I take to ignominious flight.

The Philanthropist and the Happy Cat

[**SAKI**]

Jocantha Bessbury was in the mood to be serenely and graciously happy. Her world was a pleasant place, and it was wearing one of its pleasantest aspects. Gregory had managed to get home for a hurried lunch and a smoke afterwards in the little snuggery; the lunch had been a good one, and there was just time to do justice to the coffee and cigarettes. Both were excellent in their way, and Gregory was, in his way, an excellent husband. Jocantha rather suspected herself of making him a very charming wife, and more than suspected herself of having a first-rate dressmaker.

"I don't suppose a more thoroughly contented personality is to be found in all Chelsea," observed Jocantha in allusion to herself; "except perhaps

Attab," she continued, glancing towards the large tabby-marked cat that lay in considerable ease in a corner of the divan. "He lies there, purring and dreaming, shifting his limbs now and then in an ecstasy of cushioned comfort. He seems the incarnation of everything soft and silky and velvety, without a sharp edge in his composition, a dreamer whose philosophy is sleep and let sleep; and then, as evening draws on, he goes out into the garden with a red glint in his eyes and slays a drowsy sparrow."

"As every pair of sparrows hatches out ten or more young ones in the year, while their food supply remains stationary, it is just as well that the Attabs of the community should have that idea of how to pass an amusing afternoon," said Gregory. Having delivered himself of this sage comment he lit another cigarette, bade Jocantha a playfully affectionate good-bye, and departed into the outer world.

"Remember, dinner's a wee bit earlier to-night, as we're going to the Haymarket," she called after him.

Left to herself, Jocantha continued the process of looking at her life with placid, introspective eyes. If she had not everything she wanted in this world, at least she was very well pleased with what she had got. She was very well pleased, for instance, with the snuggery, which contrived somehow to be cozy and dainty and expensive all at once. The porcelain was rare and beautiful, the Chinese enamels took on wonderful tints in the firelight, the rugs and hangings led the eye through sumptuous harmonies of coloring. It was a room in which one might have suitably entertained an ambassador or an archbishop, but it was also a room in which one could cut out pictures for a scrapbook without feeling that one was scandalizing the deities of the place with one's litter. And as with the snuggery, so with the rest of the house, and as with the house, so with the other departments of Jocantha's life; she really had good reason for being one of the most contented women in Chelsea.

From being in a mood of simmering satisfaction with her lot she passed to the phase of being generously commiserating for those thousands around her whose lives and circumstances were dull, cheap, pleasureless, and empty. Work girls, shop assistants and so forth, the class that have neither the happy-go-lucky freedom of the poor nor the leisured freedom of the rich, came specially within the range of her sympathy. It was sad to think that there were young people who, after a long day's work, had to sit alone in chill, dreary bedrooms because they could not afford the price of a cup of coffee and a sandwich in a restaurant, still less a shilling for a theatre gallery.

Jocantha's mind was still dwelling on this theme when she started forth on an afternoon campaign of desultory shopping; it would be rather a comforting thing, she told herself, if she could do something, on the spur of the moment, to bring a gleam of pleasure and interest into the life of even one or two wistful-hearted, empty-pocketed workers; it would add a good deal to her sense of enjoyment at the theatre that night. She would get two upper circle tickets for a popular play, make her way into some cheap teashop, and present the tickets to the first couple of interesting work girls with whom she could casually drop into conversation. She could explain matters by saying that she was unable to use the tickets herself and did not want them to be wasted, and, on the other hand, did not want the trouble of sending them back. On further reflection she decided that it might be better to get only one ticket and give it to some lonely-looking girl sitting eating her frugal meal by herself; the girl might scrape acquaintance with her next-seat neighbor at the theatre and lay the foundations of a lasting friendship.

With the Fairy Godmother impulse strong upon her, Jocantha marched into a ticket agency and selected with immense care an upper circle seat for the "Yellow Peacock," a play that was attracting a considerable amount of discussion and criticism. Then she went forth in search of a teashop and philanthropic adventure, at about the same time that Attab sauntered into the garden with a mind attuned to sparrow stalking. In a corner of an A.B.C. shop she found an unoccupied table, whereat she promptly installed herself, impelled by the fact that at the next table was sitting a young girl, rather plain of feature, with tired, listless eyes, and a general air of uncomplaining forlornness. Her dress was of poor material, but aimed at being in the fashion, her hair was pretty, and her complexion bad; she was finishing a modest meal of tea and scone, and she was not very different in her way from thousands of other girls who were finishing, or beginning, or continuing their teas in London teashops at that exact moment. The odds were enormously in favor of the supposition that she had never seen the "Yellow Peacock": obviously she supplied excellent material for Jocantha's first experiment in haphazard benefaction.

Jocantha ordered some tea and a muffin, and then turned a friendly scrutiny on her neighbor with a view to catching her eye. At that precise moment the girl's face lit up with sudden pleasure, her eyes sparkled, a flush came into her cheeks, and she looked almost pretty. A young man, whom she greeted with an affectionate "Hullo, Bertie," came up to her table and took his seat in a chair facing her. Jocantha looked hard at the newcomer; he was in appearance a few years younger than herself, very much better looking than Gregory, rather better looking, in fact, than any of the young men of her set. She guessed him to be a well-mannered young clerk in some wholesale warehouse, existing and amusing himself as best he might on a tiny salary, and commanding a holiday of about two weeks in the year. He was aware, of course, of his good looks, but with the shy self-consciousness of the Anglo-Saxon, not the blatant complacency of the Latin. He was obviously on terms of friendly intimacy with the girl he was talking to, probably they were drifting towards a formal engagement. Jocantha pictured the boy's home, in a rather narrow circle, with a tiresome mother who always wanted to know how and where he spent his evenings. He would exchange that humdrum thralldom in due course for a home of his own, dominated by a chronic scarcity of pounds, shillings, and pence, and a dearth of most of the things that made life attractive or comfortable. Jocantha felt extremely sorry for him. She wondered if he had seen the "Yellow Peacock": the odds were enormously in favor of the supposition that he had not. The girl had finished her tea and would shortly be going back to her work; when the boy was alone it would be quite easy for Jocantha to say: "My husband has made other arrangements for me this evening; would you care to make use of this ticket, which would otherwise be wasted?" Then she could come there again one afternoon for tea, and, if she saw him, ask him how he liked the play. If he was a nice boy and improved on acquaintance he could be given more theatre tickets, and perhaps asked to come one Sunday to tea at Chelsea. Jocantha made up her mind that he would improve on acquaintance, and that Gregory would like him, and that the Fairy Godmother business would prove far more entertaining than she had originally anticipated. The boy was distinctly presentable; he knew how to brush his hair, which was possibly an imitative faculty; he knew what color of tie suited him, which might be intuition; he was exactly the type that Jocantha admired, which of course was accident. Altogether she was rather pleased when the girl looked at the clock and bade a friendly but hurried farewell to her companion. Bertie nodded "good-bye," gulped down a mouthful of tea, and then produced from his overcoat pocket a paper-covered book, bearing the title *Sepoy and Sahib, a Tale of the Great Mutiny.*

The laws of teashop etiquette forbid that you should offer theatre tickets to a stranger without having first caught the stranger's eye. It is even better if you can ask to have a sugar basin passed to you, having previously concealed the fact that you have a large and well-filled sugar basin on your own table; this is not difficult to manage, as the printed menu is generally nearly as large as the table, and can be made to stand on end. Jocantha set to work hopefully; she had a long and rather high-pitched discussion with the waitress concerning alleged defects in an altogether blameless muffin, she made loud and plaintive inquiries about the tube service to some impossibly remote suburb, she talked with brilliant insincerity to the teashop kitten, and as a last resort she upset a milk-jug and swore at it daintily. Altogether she attracted a good deal of attention, but never for a moment did she attract the attention of the boy with the beautifully brushed hair, who was some thousands of miles away in the baking plains of Hindostan, amid deserted bungalows, seething bazaars, and riotous barrack squares, listening to the throbbing of tom-toms and the distant rattle of musketry.

Jocantha went back to her house in Chelsea, which struck her for the first time as looking dull and over-furnished. She had a resentful conviction that Gregory would be uninteresting at dinner, and that the play would be stupid after dinner. On the whole her frame of mind showed a marked divergence from the purring complacency of Attab, who was again curled up in his corner of the divan with a great peace radiating from every curve of his body.

But then he had killed his sparrow.

Plato: The Story of a Cat

[A. S. DOWNS]

One day last summer a large handsome black cat walked gravely up one side of Main Street, crossed, and went halfway down the other. He stopped at a house called The Den, went up the piazza steps, and paused by an open window.

A lady sitting inside saw and spoke to him; but without taking any notice, he put his paws on the sill, looked around the room as if wondering if it would suit him, and finally gazed into her face.

After thinking a minute he went in, and from that hour took his place as an important member of the family. Civil to all, he gives his love only to the lady whom he first saw; and it is odd to see, as he lies by the fire, how he listens to all conversation, but raises his head only when she speaks, and drops it again when she has finished, with a pleased air.

No other person in the house is so wise, for he alone never makes a mistake. The hours he selects for his exercise are the sunniest; the carpets he lies upon the softest, and he knows the moment he enters the room whether his friend will let him lie in her lap, or whether because of her best gown she will have none of him. No one at The Den can tell how he came to be called Plato. It is a fact that he answers to the name, and when asked if so known before he came there, smiles wisely. "What matters it," the smile says, "how I was called, or where I came from, since I am Plato, and am here?"

He dislikes noise, and entirely disapproves sweeping. A broom and dustpan fill him with anxiety, and he seeks the soft cushions of the big lounge; but when these in their turn are beaten and tossed about, he retreats to the study-table. However, as soon as he learned that once a week his favorite room was turned into chaos, he sought another refuge, and refuses to get up that day until noon.

Many were the speculations as to Plato's Christmas present. All were satisfied with a rattan basket just large enough for him to lie in, with a light open canopy, cushions of cardinal chintz, and a cardinal satin bow to which was fastened a lovely card.

It was set down before Plato, and although it is probable it was the first he had ever seen, he showed neither surprise nor curiosity, but looked at it loftily

as if such a retreat should have been given him long
ago, for could not any discerning person see he was
accustomed to luxury? He stepped in carefully and
curled himself gracefully upon the soft cushions, the
glowing tints of which were very becoming to his
sable beauty.

It was soon seen that Plato was very fond of his
basket, and was unwilling to share it in the smallest
degree. When little Bessie put her doll in, "just to see
if cardinal was becoming to her," he looked so stern
and walked so fiercely toward them that dolly's heart
sank within her, and Bessie said, "Please excuse us,
Plato." If balls and toys were carelessly dropped there
he would push them out without delay, and if visitors
took up the basket to examine it, he would fix his
eyes upon them, thinking, "O yes, you would pick
pockets or steal the spoons if I did not watch you."

As his conduct can never be predicted, great was
the curiosity when one cold afternoon he was
noticed walking up the avenue while a miserable
yellow kitten dragged herself after him. She was so
thin you could count her bones, and she had been so
pulled and kicked that there seemed to be nothing
of her but length and—dirt.

When Lord Plato chooses, he enters the front doors,
but as he waits no man's pleasure, unless it pleases him
first, he has a way of getting in on his own account.
Upon one of the shed doors is an old-fashioned latch,

which by jumping he can reach and lift with his paw. Having opened the door, he pushed his poor yellow straggler in and followed himself. She laid down at once on the floor, and Plato began washing her with his rough tongue, while the lookers-on assisted his hospitality by bringing a saucer of milk. While she ate, Plato rested, looking as pleased as if he were her mother at her enjoyment. The luncheon finished, the washing was resumed, and as the waif was now able to help, she soon looked more respectable. But Plato had not finished his work of mercy. He looked at the door leading to the parlor, then at her; and finally bent down tenderly to her little torn ears, as if whispering, but she would not move. Perhaps in all her wretched life she had never been so comfortable, and believed in letting well enough alone. Reason and persuasion alike useless, Plato concluded to try force and, taking her by the back of the neck, carried her through the house and dropped her close to his dainty cherished basket.

Then he appeared a little uncertain what to do. The basket was nice and warm; he was tired and cold; it had been a present to him; the street wanderer was dirty still; and the rug would be a softer bed than she had ever known. Were these his thoughts, and was it selfishness he conquered when at last he lifted the shivering homeless creature into his own beautiful nest?

A Talk with
Mark Twain's Cat,
the Owner Being Invisible

[NEW YORK TIMES, APRIL 9, 1905]

Mark Twain had lost his cat. Consumed with an attack of wanderlust, Bambino had fled from home and roamed for a day and a half. The humorist had offered a reward of $5. Then his secretary, Miss Lyon, had met Bambino on University Place and haled him home.

It was all in the papers.

Failing to understand why it shouldn't be in the papers some more, a woman from the *Times* had called at the Clemens mansion, 21 Fifth Avenue.

A man with china blue eyes and a white waistcoat opened the door for her. He opened it just half way.

Upon her request to see Mr. Clemens, he gave a start of surprise, frowned, and said:

"Mr. Clemens is asleep."

It was then 1:30 in the afternoon.

"When can I see him?" asked the woman.

"I will find out," said the servant, and shut the door upon her while he did so.

By and by he reopened it.

"He may see you," he told her, "if you come back at 5 o'clock."

It was a beautiful sunshiny day, but the woman went home, stayed indoors to rest up for this interview, and at 5 o'clock again sauntered toward the Clemens mansion.

The same man appeared. He wore the same waistcoat. He had, likewise, the same blue eyes.

"Mr. Clemens is not in now," he said, "but his secretary might see you."

"Very well," responded the woman, and stood outside the shut door once more while he searched for the secretary.

As she gazed upon Fifth Avenue, gay in the sunshine with automobiles and carriages and people enjoying themselves, she wondered vaguely if thieves were in the habit of infesting the Clemens mansion; if that was the reason they were so particular about the door.

Then it opened cautiously and the servant said:

"You may come in."

Precious privilege. The woman went in and stood in the hall as if she were a book agent. There were chairs, but she was afraid to sit down.

Presently the secretary, a nice little woman with brown eyes and old-fashioned sleeves, came down the stairs and asked her what she wanted.

"I want to see Mr. Clemens about the cat," replied the woman.

"Mr. Clemens never sees anybody—I mean any newspaper people. Besides, he is not at home."

"Then," said the woman, "may I see the cat?"

"Yes," nodded the secretary, "you may see the cat," and she ran lightly up the long stairway and came down soon with Bambino in her arms, a beautiful black silent cat with long velvety fur and luminous eyes that looked very intelligently into the face of the woman.

The secretary and the woman then sat down on a bench in the hall, and talked about the cat. The cat listened but said nothing.

"We were terribly distressed about him," cooed the secretary. "He is a great pet with Mr. Clemens. He is a year old. It is the first time he has ever run away. He lies curled up on Mr. Clemens's bed all day long."

"Does Mr. Clemens breakfast at five o'clock tea and dine on the following day?" asked the woman.

"Oh, no. He does all his writing before he gets up. That's why he gets up at 5 o'clock. Bambino always stays with him while he writes."

"I should consider it a great privilege," smiled the woman, "to breathe the same atmosphere with Mr.

Clemens for about three minutes. Don't you think if I came back at 7 you might arrange it?"

"I will try," promised the secretary, kindly.

At 7, therefore, the woman toiled up the dark red steps and rang the bell. The china-eyed man with the white waistcoat opened the door, disclosed one eye and the half of his face, said abruptly, "Mr. Clemens doesn't wish to see you," and slammed the door.

The woman walked slowly down the red steps and looked up Fifth Avenue, wondering whether she would walk home or take a car.

Fifth Avenue was very beautiful.

Purplish in the dusk, it was gemmed with softly gleaming opalescent electric balls of light.

It was, moreover, admirably bare of people.

She concluded to walk home.

She was about to start forward when she became aware of a furry gentle something rubbing against her skirts.

She looked down, and there was Bambino, purring at her, looking up at her out of his luminous cat eyes.

The man at the door had shut him out, too!

She took him in both hands and lifted him up. He nestled against her shoulder.

"I don't like to prejudice you against the people you have to live with, Bambino," she said. "It seems they will make you live with them. But they weren't so nice. Were they? They might have told me at the start he wouldn't see me. They needn't have made me lose all the sunshine of to-day. You can't bring back a day and you can't bring back sunshine.

"You wouldn't have treated me like that, would you?"

Bambino purred musically in his earnest assurance that he would not.

"I suppose you heard it all," she went on, "and you sympathized with me. You are awfully tired yourself. I can see that. If you were a Parisian cat we'd call it *ennui,* that expresses it better, but we'll let it go at tired. You are. Aren't you? Or you wouldn't have run off."

Bambino sighed wearily and half closed his eyes.

"It's a pretty rarefied atmosphere, I imagine, for a cat," she reasoned. "I don't blame you for wanting to get out with the common cats and whoop it up a little. Any self respecting cat would rather run himself in a gutter or walk the back fence than sit cooped up the livelong day with a humorist. You can't tell me anything about that. It's a deadly thing to see people grind out fun. I used to know a comic artist. I had to sit by and watch him try to match his jokes to pictures!"

She clasped Bambino closer and caught her breath in a sigh.

"I don't blame you one bit for running off," she reiterated. "I can imagine what you must have suffered. Shall we walk along a little on this beautiful street that's so wide and empty now of people?" she asked politely. "I get as tired as you do sometimes of people, Bambino. They are not always so nice. There are a lot of times that I like cats better."

Bambino curled himself up in her arms and laid an affectionate paw on her wrist by way of rewarding her.

She walked on, fondling him.

"I've the greatest notion," she confided presently, "to run off with you and paralyze them. It would serve them right. How would you like, Bambino, to come and live with me in my studio?"

Bambino raised his head and purred loudly against her cheek to show how well he would like it.

"Now, I want to tell you exactly how it will be. I want to be perfectly fair with you. If you come with me you must come with your eyes open. Maybe you won't have half as soft a bed to lie on, but you won't have to lie on it all day long. I'll promise you that. In the first place, it masquerades as a couch full of pillows in the daytime, and in the second place I've got to get out and hustle if I want to eat. Not that I mind hustling. I wouldn't stay in bed all day long out of the sunshine if I could. And you mayn't have as much to eat either, but if you get too hungry there are the goldfish—and the canary wouldn't make half a bad meal. I am pretty fond of both, but I am reckless to-night somehow. You'll be welcome to them."

Bambino licked his chops preparatorily.

"There are a good many little things you are apt to miss. The studio isn't as big as a house by any means, but you'll have all out doors to roam in. I'll trust to your coming home of nights because you'll like it there," she concluded confidently.

"And you'll be rid of the man at the door for good and all. Tell me, now, doesn't he step on your tail and 'sic' the mice on you when they are all away?"

Bambino groaned slightly, but he was otherwise noncommittal.

"I knew he did. He looks capable of anything. He's not as wise as he looks, though. He may not know it, but I push the pen for the tallest newspaper building in the city, the tallest in the world, I think. I'll take you up to the top of that building of mine, and let you climb the flag pole. Then if there should happen to be another cat on the Flatiron Building there'd be some music, wouldn't there, for the rest of the city? And they couldn't throw that flatiron at you anyway, could they? Want to go?"

Bambino put both paws around her neck, and purred an eloquent assent.

"You talk less than anybody I ever interviewed," remarked the woman, "but I think I know what you mean."

She pressed his affectionate black paws against her neck and hurried up the avenue, looking back over her shoulder to see that nobody followed.

She almost ran until she got to the bridge over the yawning chasm near Sixteenth Street. Then she stopped.

Bambino looked anxiously up to see what was the matter.

But turned deliberately around.

Bambino gave a long-drawn sigh. He looked appealingly up at her out of his luminous eyes.

"I reckon I won't steal you, Bambino," she concluded, sadly. "I'd like to, but it wouldn't be fair.

"In the morning he'd be sorry. Maybe he couldn't work without you there, looking at him out of your beautiful eyes. You don't have to hear him dictate, too, do you Bambino? If I thought that! *** But no. There is a limit. He's had his troubles, too, you know. He's bound to be a little lenient. The goose hasn't always hung so high for him. Of course you don't remember it, but he had an awful time establishing himself as the great American humorist. Couldn't get a single publisher to believe it. Had to publish his *Innocents Abroad* himself. Just said to the American public, 'Now, you've got to take this. It's humor,' and made them take it. Held their noses. That was a long time ago. Couldn't do it to-day. Not with *Innocents Abroad*. The American public is getting too well educated. Who ever reads *Innocents Abroad* now? Not the rising generation. You ask any boy of to-day what is the funniest book, and see if he doesn't say *Alice in Wonderland*?

"Still, for an old back date book, that wasn't half bad. He has never written anything better. It must give him the heartache to see it laid on the shelf. I suppose you must hear these things discussed, but not this side of them, perhaps. No. Naturally no. They don't make you read their books, they can't, but you must have to hear about them. ∗∗∗ Life is hard! But I must take you back. We mustn't do anything at all to hurt his feelings."

Bambino was fairly limp with disappointment. He had set his heart on the top of the *Times* building flagpole. He had almost tasted the canary, to say nothing of the goldfish. He hadn't the heart to purr any longer. His paws fell from the woman's neck. She had to carry him like that, all four feet handing lifeless, his head drooping.

"And there's another thing, Bambino," she continued, as they went along. "I don't want anything I said about his having to establish himself as a humorist to disillusion you or make you more dissatisfied than you are. All humorists are like that. They have to establish themselves. Why, wasn't I in London when Nat Goodwin produced his *Cowboy and the Lady* at Daly's? Couldn't I hear people he had planted all over the audience that first night explaining that he was a humorist, and the play was intended to be funny? Certainly. But it didn't work that well. Those English people are more determined than we are. They wouldn't stand for it. He had to take the play off.

"Your master happened to catch us when we were young and innocent. He deserves a lot of credit for bamboozling us. You ought to admire him for it. I do."

They were nearly home by now. Bambino managed to emit another purr. It was like a whimper.

"Don't you cry, Bambino," she soothed. "We all have our troubles. You must be a brave cat and bear up under yours," and she tiptoed up the red steps and set him at the door where they could find him when they missed him.

He sat there, a crumpled, black, discouraged ball, his eyes following her hungrily.

She ran back to him.

"Bear up under it the best you can, Bambino," she implored; "but if it gets so you can't stand it again, you know where to find a friend."

There was a sound of approaching footsteps in the hall.

She pressed her lips to Bambino's ear, whispered her address to him, and fled.

Ye Marvellous Legend of Tom Connor's Cat

[SAMUEL LOVER]

"There was a man in these parts, sir, you must know, called Tom Connor, and he had a cat that was equal to any dozen of rat-traps, and he was proud of the baste, and with rayson; for she was worth her weight in gold to him in saving his sacks of meal from the thievery of the rats and mice; for Tom was an extensive dealer in corn, and influenced the rise and fall of that article in the market, to the extent of a full dozen of sacks at a time, which he either kept or sold, as the spirit of free trade or monopoly came over him. Indeed, at one time, Tom had serious thoughts of applying to the government for a military force to protect his granary when there was a threatened famine in the county."

"Pooh! pooh! sir," said the matter-of-fact little man: "as if a dozen sacks could be of the smallest consequence in a whole county—pooh! pooh!"

"Well, sir," said Murphy, "I can't help if you don't believe; but it's truth what I am telling you, and pray don't interrupt me, though you may not believe; by the time the story's done you'll have heard more wonderful things than *that*,—and besides, remember you're a stranger in these parts, and have no notion of the extraordinary things, physical, metaphysical, and magical, which constitute the idiosyncrasy of rural destiny."

The little man did not know the meaning of Murphy's last sentence—nor Murphy either; but, having stopped the little man's throat with big words, he proceeded—

"This cat, sir, you must know, was a great pet, and was so up to everything, that Tom swore she was a'most like a Christian, only she couldn't speak, and had so sensible a look in her eyes, that he was sartin sure the cat knew every word that was said to her. Well, she used to sit by him at breakfast every morning, and the eloquent cock of her tail, as she used to rub against his leg, said, 'Give me some milk, Tom Connor,' as plain as print, and the plenitude of her purr afterwards spoke a gratitude beyond language. Well, one morning, Tom was going to the neighbouring town to market, and he had promised the wife to bring home shoes to the childre' out o' the price of the corn; and sure enough, before he sat down to breakfast, there was Tom taking the measure of the children's feet, by cutting notches on a bit of stick; and the wife gave him so many cautions about getting a 'nate fit' for 'Billy's purty feet,' that Tom, in his anxiety to nick the closest possible measure, cut off the child's toe. That disturbed the harmony of the party, and Tom was obliged to breakfast alone, while the mother was endeavouring to cure Billy; in short, trying to make a *heel* of his *toe.* Well, sir, all the time Tom was taking measure for the shoes, the cat was observing him with that luminous peculiarity of eye for which her tribe is remarkable; and when Tom sat down to breakfast the cat rubbed up against him more vigorously than usual; but Tom, being bewildered between his expected gain in corn and the positive loss of his child's toe, kept never minding her, until the cat, with a sort of caterwauling growl, gave Tom a dab of her claws, that went clean through his leathers, and a little further. 'Wow!' says Tom, with a jump, clapping his hand on the part, and rubbing it, 'by this and that, you drew the blood out o' me,' says Tom; 'you wicked divil—tish!—go along!' says he, making a kick at her. With that the cat gave a reproachful look at him, and her eyes glared just like a pair of mail-coach lamps in a fog. With that, sir, the cat, with a mysterious *'mi-ow'* fixed a most penetrating glance on Tom, and distinctly uttered his name.

"Tom felt every hair on his head as stiff as a pump-handle; and scarcely crediting his ears, he returned a searching look at the cat, who very quietly proceeded in a sort of nasal twang—

"'Tom Connor,' says she.

"'The Lord be good to me!' says Tom, 'if it isn't spakin' she is!'

"'Tom Connor,' says she again.

"'Yes, ma'am,' says Tom.

"'Come here,' says she; 'whisper—I want to talk to you, Tom,' says she, 'the laste taste in private,' says she—rising on her hams, and beckoning him with her paw out o' the door, with a wink and a toss o' the head aiqual to a milliner.

"Well, as you may suppose, Tom didn't know whether he was on his head or his heels, but he followed the cat, and off she went and squatted herself under the edge of a little paddock at the back of Tom's house; and as he came round the corner, she held up her paw again, and laid it on her mouth, as much as to say, 'Be cautious, Tom.' Well, divil a word Tom could say at all, with the fright, so up he goes to the cat, and says she—

"'Tom,' says she, 'I have a great respect for you, and there's something I must tell you, becase you're losing character with your neighbours,' says she, 'by your goin's on,' says she, 'and it's out o' the respect that I have for you, that I must tell you,' says she.

"'Thank you, ma'am,' says Tom.

"'You're goin' off to the town,' says she, 'to buy shoes for the childre',' says she, 'and never thought o' gettin' me a pair.'

"'You!' says Tom."

"'Yis, me, Tom Connor,' says she; 'and the neighbours wondhers that a respectable man like you allows your cat to go about the counthry barefutted,' says she."

"'Is it a cat to ware shoes?' says Tom."

"'Why not?' says she; 'doesn't horses ware shoes?—and I have a prettier foot than a horse, I hope,' says she, with a toss of her head."

"'Faix, she spakes like a woman; so proud of her feet,' says Tom to himself, astonished, as you may suppose, but pretending never to think it remarkable all the time; and so he went on discoursin'; and says he, 'It's thrue for you, ma'am,' says he, 'that horses wares shoes—but that stands to rayson, ma'am, you see—seeing the hardship their feet has to go through on the hard roads.'"

"'And how do you know what hardship my feet has to go through?' says the cat, mighty sharp."

"'But, ma'am,' says Tom, 'I don't well see how you could fasten a shoe on you,' says he."

"'Lave that to me,' says the cat."

"'Did any one ever stick walnut shells on you, pussy?' says Tom, with a grin."

"'Don't be disrespectful, Tom Connor,' says the cat, with a frown."

"'I ax your pard'n, ma'am,' says he, 'but as for the horses you wor spakin' about wearin' shoes, you know their shoes is fastened on with nails, and how would your shoes be fastened on?'"

"'Ah, you stupid thief!' says she, 'haven't I illigant nails o' my own?' and with that she gave him a dab of her claw, that made him roar."

"'Ow! murdher!' says he."

"'Now, no more of your palaver, Misther Connor,' says the cat; 'just be off and get me the shoes.'"
"'Tare an' ouns!' says Tom, 'what'll become o' me if I'm to get shoes for my cats?' says he, 'for you increase your family four times a year, and you have six or seven every time,' says he; 'and then you must all have two pair a piece—wirra! wirra!—I'll be ruined in shoe-leather,' says Tom.

"'No more o' your stuff,' says the cat; 'don't be stand in' here undher the hedge talkin', or we'll lose our karacthers—for I've remarked your wife is jealous, Tom.'

"'Pon my sowl, that's thrue,' says Tom, with a smirk.

"'More fool she,' says the cat, 'for, 'pon my conscience, Tom, you're as ugly as if you wor bespoke.'

"Off ran the cat with these words, leaving Tom in amazement. He said nothing to the family, for fear of fright'ning them, and off he went to the *town* as he *pretended*—for he saw the cat watching him through a hole in the hedge; but when he came to a turn at the end of the road, the dickings a mind he minded the market, good or bad, but went off to Squire Botherum's, the magisthrit, to sware examinations agen the cat."

"Pooh! pooh!—nonsense!!" broke in the little man, who had listened thus far to Murtough with an expression of mingled wonder and contempt, while the rest of the party willingly gave up the reins to nonsense, and enjoyed Murtough's Legend and their companion's more absurd common sense.

"Don't interrupt him, Goggins," said Mister Wiggins.

"How can you listen to such nonsense?" returned Goggins. "Swear examinations against a cat, indeed! pooh! pooh!"

"My dear sir," said Murtough, "remember this is a fair story, and that the country all around here is full of enchantment. As I was telling you, Tom went off to swear examinations."

"Ay, ay!" shouted all but Goggins; "go on with the story."

"And when Tom was asked to relate the events of the morning, which brought him before Squire

Botherum, his brain was so bewildered between his corn, and his cat, and his child's toe, that he made a very confused account of it.

"'Begin your story from the beginning,' said the magistrate to Tom.

"'Well, your honour,' says Tom, 'I was goin' to market this mornin', to sell the child's corn—I beg your pard'n—my own toes, I mane, sir.'

"'Sell your toes!' said the Squire.

"'No, sir, takin' the cat to market, I mane—'

"'Take a cat to market!' said the Squire. 'You're drunk, man.'

"'No, your honour, only confused a little; for when the toes began to spake to me—the cat, I mane—I was bothered clane—'

"'The cat speak to you!' said the Squire. 'Phew! worse than before—you're drunk, Tom.'

"'No, your honour; it's on the strength of the cat I come to spake to you—'

"'I think it's on the strength of a pint of whisky, Tom—'

"'By the vartue o' my oath, your honour, it's nothin' but the cat.' And so Tom then told him all about the affair, and the Squire was regularly astonished. Just then the bishop of the diocese and the priest of the parish happened to call in, and heard the story; and the bishop and the priest had a tough argument for two hours on the subject; the former swearing she must be a witch; but the priest denying *that,* and maintaining she was *only* enchanted; and that part of the argument was afterwards referred to the primate, and subsequently to the conclave at Rome; but the Pope declined interfering about cats, saying he had quite enough to do minding his own bulls.

"'In the meantime, what are we to do with the cat?' says Botherum.

"'Burn her,' says the bishop, 'she's a witch.'

"'*Only* enchanted,' said the priest—'and the ecclesiastical court maintains that—'

"'Bother the ecclesiastical court!' said the magistrate; 'I can only proceed on the statutes'; and with that he pulled down all the law-books in his library, and hunted the laws from Queen Elizabeth down, and he found that they made laws against everything in Ireland, *except a cat.* The devil a thing escaped them but a cat, which did *not* come within the meaning of any act of parliament:—*the cats only had escaped.*

"'There's the alien act, to be sure,' said the magistrate, 'and perhaps she's a French spy, in disguise.'

"'She spakes like a French spy, sure enough,' says Tom; 'and she was missin', I remember, all last Spy-Wednesday.'

"'That's suspicious,' says the squire—'but conviction might be difficult; and I have a fresh idea,' says Botherum.

"'Faith, it won't keep fresh long, this hot weather,' says Tom; 'so your honour had betther make use of it at wanst.'

"'Right,' says Botherum,—'we'll make her subject to the game laws; we'll hunt her,' says he.

"'Ow!—elegant!' says Tom;—'we'll have a brave run out of her.'

"'Meet me at the cross roads,' says the Squire, 'in the morning, and I'll have the hounds ready.'

"Well, off Tom went home; and he was racking his brain what excuse he could make to the cat for not bringing the shoes; and at last he hit one off, just as he saw her cantering up to him, half-a-mile before he got home.

"'Where's the shoes, Tom?' says she.

"'I have not got them to-day, ma'am,' says he.

"'Is that the way you keep your promise, Tom?' says she;—'I'll tell you what it is, Tom—I'll tare the eyes out o' the childre' if you don't get me shoes.'

"'Whisht! whisht!' says Tom, frightened out of his life for his children's eyes. 'Don't be in a passion, pussy. The shoemaker said he had not a shoe in his shop, nor a last that would make one to fit you; and he says, I must bring you into the town for him to take your measure.'

"'And when am I to go?' says the cat, looking savage.

"'To-morrow,' says Tom.

"'It's well you said that, Tom,' said the cat, 'or the devil an eye I'd leave in your family this night'—and off she hopped.

"Tom thrimbled at the wicked look she gave.

"'Remember!' says she, over the hedge, with a bitter caterwaul.

"'Never fear,' says Tom. Well, sure enough, the next mornin' there was the cat at cock-crow, licking herself as nate as a new pin, to go into the town, and out came Tom with a bag undher his arm, and the cat afther him.

"'Now git into this, and I'll carry you into the town,' says Tom, opening the bag.

"'Sure I can walk with you,' says the cat.

"'Oh, that wouldn't do,' says Tom; 'the people in the town is curious and slandherous people, and sure it would rise ugly remarks if I was seen with a cat afther me:—a dog is a man's companion by nature, but cats does not stand to rayson.'

"Well, the cat, seeing there was no use in argument, got into the bag, and off Tom set to the cross roads with the bag over his shoulder, and he came up, *quite innocent-like,* to the corner, where the Squire, and his huntsman, and the hounds, and a pack o' people were waitin'. Out came the Squire on a sudden, just as if it was all by accident.

"'God save you, Tom,' says he.

"'God save you kindly, sir,' says Tom.

"'What's that bag you have at your back?' says the Squire.

"'Oh, nothin' at all, sir,' says Tom—makin' a face all the time, as much as to say, I have her safe.

"'Oh, there's something in that bag, I think,' says the Squire; 'and you must let me see it.'

"'If you bethray me, Tom Connor,' says the cat in a low voice, 'by this and that I'll never spake to you again!'

"'Pon my honour, sir,' said Tom, with a wink and a twitch of his thumb towards the bag, 'I haven't anything in it.'

"'I have been missing my praties of late,' says the Squire; 'and I'd just like to examine that bag,' says he.

"'Is it doubting my charackther you'd be, sir?' says Tom, pretending to be in a passion.

"'Tom, your sowl!' says the voice in the sack, '*if you let the cat out of the bag,* I'll murther you.'

"'An honest man would make no objection to be sarched,' said the Squire; 'and I insist on it,' says he, laying hold o' the bag, and Tom purtending to fight all the time; but, my jewel! before two minutes, they shook the cat out o' the bag, sure enough, and off she went with her tail as big as a sweeping brush, and the Squire, with a thundering view halloo after her, clapt the dogs at her heels, and away they went for the bare life. Never was there seen such running as that day—the cat made for a shaking bog, the loneliest place in the whole country, and there the riders were all thrown out, barrin' the huntsman, who had a web-footed horse on purpose for soft places; and the priest, whose horse could go any-where by reason of the priest's blessing; and, sure enough, the huntsman and his riverence stuck to the hunt like wax; and just as the cat got on the border of the bog, they saw her give a twist as the foremost dog closed with her, for he gave her a nip in the flank. Still she went on, however, and headed them well, towards an old mud cabin in the middle of the bog, and there they saw her jump in at the window, and up came the dogs the next minit, and gathered round the house with the most horrid howling ever was heard. The huntsman alighted, and went into the house to turn the cat out again, when what should he see but an old hag lying in bed in the corner?

"'Did you see a cat come in here?' says he.

"'Oh, no—o—o—o!' squealed the old hag, in a trembling voice; 'there's no cat here,' says she.

"'Yelp, yelp, yelp!' went the dogs outside.

"'Oh, keep the dogs out o' this,' says the old hag—'oh—o—o—o!' and the huntsman saw her eyes glare under the blanket, just like a cat's.

"'Hillo!' says the huntsman, pulling down the blanket—and what should he see but the old hag's flank all in a gore of blood.

"'Ow, ow! you old divil—is it you? you ould cat!' says he, opening the door.

"In rushed the dogs—up jumped the old hag, and changing into a cat before their eyes, out she darted through the window again, and made another run for it; but she couldn't escape, and the dogs gobbled her while you could say 'Jack Robinson.' But the most remarkable part of this extraordinary story, gentlemen, is, that the pack was ruined from that day out; for after having eaten the enchanted cat, *the devil a thing they would ever hunt afterwards but mice.*"

The Cat and the King

[AMBROSE BIERCE]

A cat was looking at a King, as permitted by proverb.

"Well," said the monarch, observing her inspection of the royal person, "how do you like me?"

"I can imagine a King," said the Cat, "whom I should like better."

"For example?"

"The King of the Mice."

The sovereign was so pleased with the wit of the reply that he gave her permission to scratch his Prime Minister's eyes out.

The Master Cat, or, Puss in Boots

[**CHARLES PERRAULT**]

There was a miller who left no more estate to the three sons he had than his mill his ass and his cat. The partition was soon made. Neither scrivener nor attorney was sent for. They would soon have eaten up all the poor patrimony. The eldest had the mill, the second the ass, and the youngest nothing but the cat.

The poor young fellow was quite comfortless at having so poor a lot.

"My brothers," said he, "may get their living handsomely enough by joining their stocks together; but for my part, when I have eaten up my cat, and made me a muff of his skin, I must die of hunger."

The Cat, who heard all this, but made as if he did not, said to him with a grave and serious air:

"Do not thus afflict yourself, my good master. You have nothing else to do but to give me a bag and get a pair of boots made for me that I may scamper through the dirt and the brambles, and you shall see that you have not so bad a portion in me as you imagine."

The Cat's master did not build very much upon what he said. He had often seen him play a great many cunning tricks to catch rats and mice, as when he used to hang by the heels, or hide himself in the meal, and make as if he were dead; so that he did not altogether despair of his affording him some help in his miserable condition. When the Cat had what he asked for he booted himself very gallantly, and putting his bag about his neck, he held the strings of it in his two forepaws and went into a warren where was great abundance of rabbits. He put bran and sow-thistle into his bag, and stretching out at length, as if he had been dead, he waited for some young rabbits, not yet acquainted with the deceits of the world, to come and rummage his bag for what he had put into it.

Scarce was he lain down but he had what he wanted. A rash and foolish young rabbit jumped into his bag, and Monsieur Puss, immediately drawing close the strings, took and killed him without pity. Proud of his prey, he went with it to the palace and asked to speak with his majesty. He was shown upstairs into the King's apartment, and, making a low reverence, said to him:

"I have brought you, sir, a rabbit of the warren, which my noble lord the Marquis of Carabas" (for that was the title which puss was pleased to give his master) "has commanded me to present to your majesty from him."

"Tell thy master," said the king, "that I thank him and that he does me a great deal of pleasure."

Another time he went and hid himself among some standing corn, holding still his bag open, and when a brace of partridges ran into it he drew the strings and so caught them both. He went and made a present of these to the king, as he had done before of the rabbit that he took in the warren. The king, in like manner, received the partridges with great pleasure, and ordered him some money for drink.

The Cat continued for two or three months thus to carry his Majesty, from time to time, game of his master's taking. One day in particular, when he knew for certain that he was to take the air along the river-side, with his daughter, the most beautiful princess in the world, he said to his master:

"If you will follow my advice your fortune is made. You have nothing else to do but go and wash yourself in the river, in that part I shall show you, and leave the rest to me."

The Marquis of Carabas did what the Cat advised him to, without knowing why or wherefore. While he was washing the King passed by, and the Cat began to cry out:

"Help! help! My Lord Marquis of Carabas is going to be drowned."

At this noise the King put his head out of the coach-window, and, finding it was the Cat who had so often brought him such good game, he commanded his guards to run immediately to the assistance of his Lordship the Marquis of Carabas.

While they were drawing the poor Marquis out of the river, the Cat came up to the coach and told the King that, while his master was washing, there came by some rogues, who went off with his clothes, though he had cried out: "Thieves! thieves!" several times, as loud as he could.

This cunning Cat had hidden them under a great stone. The King immediately commanded the officers of his wardrobe to run and fetch one of his best suits for the Lord Marquis of Carabas.

The King caressed him after a very extraordinary manner, and as the fine clothes he had given him extremely set off his good mien (for he was well made and very handsome in his person), the King's daughter took a secret inclination to him, and the Marquis of Carabas had no sooner cast two or three respectful and somewhat tender glances but she fell in love with him to distraction. The King would needs have him come into the coach and take part of the airing. The Cat, quite overjoyed to see his project begin to succeed, marched on before, and, meeting with some countrymen, who were mowing a meadow, he said to them:

"Good people, you who are mowing, if you do not tell the King that the meadow you mow belongs to my Lord Marquis of Carabas, you shall be chopped as small as herbs for the pot."

The King did not fail asking of the mowers to whom the meadow they were mowing belonged.

"To my Lord Marquis of Carabas," answered they altogether, for the Cat's threats had made them terribly afraid.

"You see, sir," said the Marquis, "this is a meadow which never fails to yield a plentiful harvest every year."

The Master Cat, who went still on before, met with some reapers, and said to them:

"Good people, you who are reaping, if you do not tell the King that all this corn belongs to the Marquis of Carabas, you shall be chopped as small as herbs for the pot."

The King, who passed by a moment after, would needs know to whom all that corn, which he then saw, did belong.

"To my Lord Marquis of Carabas," replied the reapers, and the King was very well pleased with it, as well as the Marquis, whom he congratulated thereupon. The Master Cat, who went always before, said the same words to all he met, and the King was astonished at the vast estates of my Lord Marquis of Carabas.

Monsieur Puss came at last to a stately castle, the master of which was an ogre, the richest had ever been known; for all the lands which the King had then gone over belonged to this castle. The Cat, who had taken care to inform himself who this ogre was and what he could do, asked to speak with him, saying he could not pass so near his castle without having the honor of paying his respects to him.

The ogre received him as civilly as an ogre could do, and made him sit down.

"I have been assured," said the Cat, "that you have the gift of being able to change yourself into all sorts of creatures you have a mind to; you can, for example, transform yourself into a lion, or elephant, and the like."

"That is true," answered the ogre very briskly; "and to convince you, you shall see me now become a lion."

Puss was so sadly terrified at the sight of a lion so near him that he immediately got into the gutter, not without abundance of trouble and danger, because of his boots, which were of no use at all to him in walking upon the tiles. A little while after, when Puss saw that the ogre had resumed his natural form, he came down, and owned he had been very much frightened.

"I have been, moreover, informed," said the Cat, "but I know not how to believe it, that you have also the power to take on you the shape of the smallest animals; for example, to change yourself into a rat or a mouse; but I must own to you I take this to be impossible."

"Impossible!" cried the ogre; "you shall see that presently."

And at the same time he changed himself into a mouse, and began to run about the floor. Puss no sooner perceived this but he fell upon him and ate him up.

Meanwhile the King, who saw, as he passed, this fine castle of the ogre's, had a mind to go into it. Puss, who heard the noise of his Majesty's coach running over the draw-bridge, ran out, and said to the King:

"Your Majesty is welcome to this castle of my Lord Marquis of Carabas."

"What! my Lord Marquis," cried the King, "and does this castle also belong to you? There can be nothing finer than this court and all the stately buildings which surround it; let us go into it, if you please."

The Marquis gave his hand to the Princess, and followed the King, who went first. They passed into a spacious hall, where they found a magnificent collation, which the ogre had prepared for his friends, who were that very day to visit him, but dared not to enter, knowing the King was there. His Majesty was perfectly charmed with the good qualities of my Lord Marquis of Carabas, as was his daughter, who had fallen violently in love with him, and, seeing the vast estate he possessed, said to him, after having drunk five or six glasses:

"It will be owing to yourself only, my Lord Marquis, if you are not my son-in-law."

The Marquis, making several low bows, accepted the honor which his Majesty conferred upon him, and forthwith, that very same day, married the Princess.

Puss became a great lord, and never ran after mice any more but only for his diversion.

How a Cat Played Robinson Crusoe

[CHARLES G. D. ROBERTS]

The island was a mere sandbank off the low, flat coast. Not a tree broke its bleak levels— not even a shrub. But the long, gritty stalks of the marsh grass clothed it everywhere above tide-mark; and a tiny rivulet of sweet water, flowing from a spring at its centre, drew a ribbon of inland herbage and tenderer green across the harsh and sombre yellow grey of the grass. Few would have chosen the island as a place to live, yet at its seaward end, where the changing tides were never still, stood a spacious, one-storied, wide-verandaed cottage, with a low shed behind it. The virtue of this lone plot of sand was coolness. When the neighbour mainland would be sweltering day and night alike under a breathless heat, out here on the island there was always a cool wind blowing. Therefore a wise city dweller had appropriated the sea waif and built his summer home thereon, where the tonic airs might bring back the rose to the pale cheeks of his children.

The family came to the island toward the end of June. In the first week of September they went away, leaving every door and window of house and shed securely shuttered, bolted or barred against the winter's storms. A roomy boat, rowed by two fishermen, carried them across the half mile of racing tides that separated them from the mainland. The elders of the household were not sorry to get back to the world of men, after two months of mere wind, and sun, and waves, and waving grass tops. But the children went with tear-stained faces. They were leaving behind them their favourite pet, the accustomed comrade of their migrations, a handsome, moon-faced cat, striped like a tiger. The animal had mysteriously disappeared two days before, vanishing from the face of the island without leaving a trace behind. The only reasonable explanation seemed to be that she had been snapped up by a passing eagle. The cat, meanwhile, was a fast prisoner at the other end of the island, hidden beneath a broken barrel and some hundred-weight of drifted sand.

The old barrel, with the staves battered out of one side, had stood, half buried, on the crest of a sand

ridge raised by a long prevailing wind. Under its lee
the cat had found a sheltered hollow, full of sun,
where she had been wont to lie curled up for hours
at a time, basking and sleeping. Meanwhile the sand
had been steadily piling itself higher and higher
behind the unstable barrier. At last it had piled too
high; and suddenly, before a stronger gust, the barrel
had come toppling over beneath a mass of sand,
burying the sleeping cat out of sight and light. But
at the same time the sound half of the barrel had
formed a safe roof to her prison, and she was neither
crushed nor smothered. When the children in their
anxious search all over the island chanced upon the
mound of fine, white sand they gave it but one care-
less look. They could not hear the faint cries that
came, at intervals, from the close darkness within. So
they went away sorrowfully, little dreaming that their
friend was imprisoned almost beneath their feet.

For three days the prisoner kept up her appeals for
help. On the third day the wind changed and
presently blew up a gale. In a few hours it had uncovered the barrel. At one corner a tiny spot of light
appeared.

Eagerly the cat stuck her paw through the hole.
When she withdrew it again the hole was much
enlarged. She took the hint and fell to scratching. At
first her efforts were rather aimless; but presently,
whether by good luck or quick sagacity, she learned

to make her scratching more effective. The opening rapidly enlarged, and at last she was able to squeeze her way out.

The wind was tearing madly across the island, filled with flying sand. The seas hurled themselves trampling up the beach, with the uproar of a bombardment. The grasses lay bowed flat in long quivering ranks. Over the turmoil the sun stared down from a deep, unclouded blue. The cat, when first she met the full force of the gale, was fairly blown off her feet. As soon as she could recover herself she crouched low and darted into the grasses for shelter. But there was little shelter there, the long stalks being held down almost level. Through their lashed lines, however, she sped straight before the gale, making for the cottage at the other end of the island, where she would find, as she fondly imagined, not only food and shelter but also loving comfort to make her forget her terrors.

Still and desolate in the bright sunshine and the tearing wind, the house frightened her. She could not understand the tight-closed shutters, the blind, unresponding doors that would no longer open to her anxious appeal. The wind swept her savagely across the naked veranda. Climbing with difficulty to the dining-room windowsill, where so often she had been let in, she clung there a few moments and yowled heartbrokenly. Then, in a sudden panic, she jumped down and ran to the shed. That, too, was closed. Never before had she seen the shed doors closed, and she could not understand it. Cautiously she crept around the foundations—but those had been built honestly: there was no such thing as getting in that way. On every side it was nothing but a blank, forbidding face that the old familiar house confronted her with.

The cat had always been so coddled and pampered by the children that she had had no need to forage for herself; but, fortunately for her, she had learned to hunt the marsh mice and grass sparrows for amusement. So now, being ravenous from her long fast under the sand, she slunk mournfully away from the deserted house and crept along under the lee of a sand ridge to a little grassy hollow which she knew. Here the gale caught only the tops of the grasses; and here, in the warmth and comparative calm, the furry little marsh folk, mice and shrews, were going about their business undisturbed.

The cat, quick and stealthy, soon caught one and eased her hunger. She caught several. And then, making her way back to the house, she spent hours in heartsick prowling around it and around, sniffing and peering, yowling piteously on the threshold and windowsill; and every now and then being blown ignominiously across the smooth, naked expanse of the veranda floor. At last, hopelessly discouraged, she curled herself up beneath the children's window and went to sleep.

In spite of her loneliness and grief the life of the island prisoner during the next two or three weeks was by no means one of hardship. Besides her abundant food of birds and mice she quickly learned to catch tiny fish in the mouth of the rivulet, where salt water and fresh water met. It was an exciting game, and she became expert at dashing the grey tom-cod and blue-and-silver sand-lance far up the slope with a sweep of her armed paw. But when the equinoctial storms roared down upon the island, with furious rain, and low, black clouds torn to shreds, then life became more difficult for her. Game all took to cover, where it was hard to find. It was difficult to get around in the drenched and lashing grass; and, moreover, she loathed wet. Most of the time she went hungry, sitting sullen and desolate under the lee of the house, glaring out defiantly at the rush and battling tumult of the waves.

The storm lasted nearly ten days before it blew itself clean out. On the eighth day the abandoned wreck of a small Nova Scotia schooner drove ashore, battered out of all likeness to a ship. But hulk as it was it had passengers of a sort. A horde of rats got through the surf and scurried into the hiding of the grass roots. They promptly made themselves at home, burrowing under the grass and beneath old, half-buried timbers, and carrying panic into the ranks of the mice and shrews.

When the storm was over the cat had a decided surprise in her first long hunting expedition. Something had rustled the grass heavily and she trailed it, expecting a particularly large, fat marsh mouse. When she pounced and alighted upon an immense old ship's rat, many-voyaged and many-battled, she got badly bitten. Such an experience had never before fallen to her lot. At first she felt so injured that she was on the point of backing out and running away. Then her latent pugnacity awoke, and the fire of far-off ancestors. She flung herself into the fight with a rage that took no accounting of the wounds she got; and the struggle was soon over. Her wounds, faithfully licked, quickly healed themselves in that clean and tonic air; and after that, having learned how to handle such big game, she no more got bitten.

During the first full moon after her abandonment—the first week in October—the island was visited by still weather with sharp night frosts. The cat discovered then that it was most exciting to hunt by night and do her sleeping in the daytime. She found that now, under the strange whiteness of the moon, all her game was astir—except the birds, which had fled to the mainland during the storm, gathering for the southward flight. The blanched grasses, she found, were now everywhere a-rustle;

and everywhere dim little shapes went darting with thin squeaks across ghostly-white sands. Also she made the acquaintaince of a new bird, which she regarded at first uneasily and then with vengeful wrath. This was the brown marsh owl, which came over from the mainland to do some autumn mouse hunting. There were two pairs of these big, downy-winged, round-eyed hunters, and they did not know there was a cat on the island.

The cat, spying one of them as it swooped sound-lessly hither and thither over the silvered grass tops, crouched with flattened ears. With its wide spread of wing it looked bigger than herself; and the great round face, with hooked beak and wild, staring eyes, appeared extremely formidable. However, she was no coward; and presently, though not without rea-sonable caution, she went about her hunting. Suddenly the owl caught a partial glimpse of her in the grass—probably of her ears or head. He swooped; and at the same instant she sprang upward to meet the assault, spitting and growling harshly and striking with unsheathed claws. With a frantic flap-ping of his great wings the owl checked himself and drew back into the air, just escaping the clutch of those indignant claws. After that the marsh owls were careful to give her a wide berth. They realized that the black-striped animal with the quick spring and the clutching claws was not to be interfered with. They perceived that she was some relation to that ferocious prowler, the lynx.

In spite of all this hunting, however, the furry life of the marsh grass was so teeming, so inexhaustible, that the depredations of cat, rats and owls were powerless to make more than a passing impression upon it. So the hunting and the merry-making went on side by side under the indifferent moon.

As the winter deepened—with bursts of sharp cold and changing winds that forced the cat to be continually changing her refuge—she grew more and more unhappy. She felt her homelessness keenly. Nowhere on the whole island could she find a nook where she might feel secure from both wind and rain. As for the old barrel, the first cause of her misfortunes, there was no help in that. The winds had long ago turned it completely over, open to the sky, then drifted it full of sand and reburied it. And in any case the cat would have been afraid to go near it again. So it came about that she alone of all the island dwellers had no shelter to turn to when the real winter arrived, with snows that smothered the grass tops out of sight, and frosts that lined the shore with grinding ice cakes. The rats had their holes under the buried fragments of wreckage; the mice and shrews had their deep, warm tunnels; the owls had nests in hollow trees far away in the forests of the mainland. But the cat, shivering and frightened, could do nothing but crouch against the blind walls of the unrelenting house and let the snow whirl itself and pile itself about her.

And now, in her misery, she found her food cut off. The mice ran secure in their hidden runways, where the grass roots on each side of them gave them easy and abundant provender. The rats, too, were out of sight—digging burrows themselves in the soft snow in the hope of intercepting some of the tunnels of the mice, and now and then snapping up an unwary passer-by. The ice fringe, crumbling and heaving under the ruthless tide, put an end to her fishing. She would have tried to capture one of the formidable owls in her hunger, but the owls no longer came to the island. They would return, no doubt, later in the season when the snow had hardened and the mice had begun to come out and play on the surface. But for the present they were following an easier chase in the deeps of the upland forest.

When the snow stopped falling and the sun came out again there fell such keen cold as the cat had never felt before. The day, as it chanced, was Christmas; and if the cat had had any idea as to the calendar she would certainly have marked the day in her memory as it was an eventful one for her. Starving as she was she could not sleep, but kept ceaselessly on the prowl. This was fortunate, for had she gone to sleep without any more shelter than the wall of the house she would never have wakened again. In her restlessness she wandered to the farther side of the island where, in a somewhat sheltered and sunny recess of the shore facing the mainland, she found a patch of bare sand, free of ice cakes and just uncovered by the tide. Opening upon this recess were the tiny entrances to several of the mouse tunnels.

Close beside one of these holds in the snow the cat crouched, quiveringly intent. For ten minutes or more she waited, never so much as twitching a whisker. At last a mouse thrust out its little pointed head. Not daring to give it time to change its mind or take alarm, she pounced. The mouse, glimpsing the doom ere it fell, doubled back upon itself in the narrow runway. Hardly realizing what she did in her desperation the cat plunged head and shoulders into the snow, reaching blindly after the vanished prize. By great good luck she caught it.

It was her first meal in four bitter days. The children had always tried to share with her their Christmas cheer and enthusiasm, and had usually succeeded in interesting her by an agreeable lavishness in the matter of cream; but never before had she found a Christmas feast so good.

Now she had learned a lesson. Being naturally clever and her wits sharpened by her fierce necessities, she had grasped the idea that it was possible to follow her prey a little way into the snow. She had not realized that the snow was so penetrable. She had quite wiped out the door of this particular runway; so she went and crouched beside a similar one, but here she had to wait a long time before an adventurous mouse came to peer out. But this time she showed that she had grasped her lesson. It was straight at the side of the entrance that she pounced, where instinct told her that the body of the mouse would be. One outstretched paw thus cut off the quarry's retreat. Her tactics were completely successful; and as her head went plunging into the fluffy whiteness she felt the prize between her paws.

Her hunger now fairly appeased, she found herself immensely excited over this new fashion of hunting. Often before had she waited at mouse holes, but never had she found it possible to break down the walls and invade the holes themselves. It was a thrilling idea. As she crept toward another hole a mouse scurried swiftly up the sand and darted into it. The cat, too late to catch him before he disappeared, tried to follow him. Scratching clumsily but hopefully she succeeded in forcing the full length of her body into the snow. She found no sign of the fugitive, which was by this time racing in safety down some dim transverse tunnel. Her eyes, mouth, whiskers and fur full of the powdery white particles, she backed out, much disappointed. But in that moment she had realized that it was much warmer in there beneath the snow than out in the stinging air. It was a second and vitally important lesson; and though she was probably unconscious of having learned it she instinctively put the new lore into practice a little while later.

Having succeeded in catching yet another mouse for which her appetite made no immediate demand, she carried it back to the house and laid it down in tribute on the veranda steps while she meowed and stared hopefully at the desolate, snow-draped door. Getting no response she carried the mouse down with her to the hollow behind the drift which had been caused by the bulging front of the bay-window on the end of the house. Here she curled herself up forlornly, thinking to have a wink of sleep.

But the still cold was too searching. She looked at the sloping wall of snow beside her and cautiously thrust her paw into it. It was very soft and light. It seemed to offer practically no resistance. She pawed away in an awkward fashion till she had scooped out a sort of tiny cave. Gently she pushed herself into it, pressing back the snow on every side till she had room to turn around.

Then turn around she did several times, as dogs do in getting their beds arranged to their liking. In this process she not only packed down the snow beneath her, but she also rounded out for herself a snug chamber with a comparatively narrow doorway. From this snowy retreat she gazed forth with a solemn air of possession; then she went to sleep with a sense of comfort, of 'homeyness', such as she had never before felt since the disappearance of her friends.

Having thus conquered misfortune and won herself the freedom of the winter wild, her life though strenuous was no longer one of any terrible hardship. With patience at the mouse holes she could catch enough to eat; and in her snowy den she slept warm and secure. In a little while, when a crust had formed over the surface, the mice took to coming out at night and holding revels on the snow. Then the owls, too, came back; and the cat, having tried to catch one, got sharply bitten and clawed before she realized the propriety of letting it go. After this experience she decided that owls, on the whole, were meant to be let alone. But for all that she found it fine hunting, out there on the bleak, unfenced, white reaches of the snow.

Thus, mistress of the situation, she found the winter slipping by without further serious trials. Only once, toward the end of January, did Fate send her another bad quarter of an hour. On the heels of a peculiarly bitter cold snap a huge white owl from the Arctic Barrens came one night to the island. The cat, taking observations from the corner of the veranda, caught sight of him. One look was enough to assure her that this was a very different kind of visitor from the brown marsh owls. She slipped inconspicuously down into her burrow; and until the great white owl went away, some twenty-four hours later, she kept herself discreetly out of sight.

When spring came back to the island, with the nightly shrill chorus of fluting frogs in the shallow, sedgy pools and the young grass alive with nesting birds, the prisoner's life became almost luxurious in its easy abundance. But now she was once more homeless, since her snug den had vanished with the snow. This did not much matter to her, how-ever, for the weather grew warmer and more tran-quil day by day; and moreover, she herself, in being forced back upon her instincts, had learned to be as contented as a tramp. Nevertheless, with all her capacity for learning and adapting herself she had not forgotten anything. So when, one day in June, a crowded boat came over from the mainland, and children's voices, clamouring across the grass tops, broke the desolate silence of the island, the cat heard and sprang up out of her sleep on the veranda steps.

For one second she stood, listening intently. Then, almost as a dog would have done, and as few of her supercilious tribe ever condescend to do, she went racing across to the landing place—to be snatched up into the arms of four happy children at once, and to have her fine fur ruffled to a state which it would cost her an hour's assiduous toilet to put in order.

The Yellow Terror

[W. L. ALDEN]

"Speaking of cats," said Captain Foster, "I'm free to say that I don't like 'em. I don't care to be looked down on by any person, whether he be man or cat. I know I ain't the President of the United States, nor yet a millionaire, nor yet the Boss of New York, but all the same I calculate that I'm a man, and entitled to be treated as such. Now, I never knew a cat yet that didn't look down on me, same as cats do on everybody. A cat considers that men are just dirt under his or her paws, as the case may be. I can't see what it is that makes a cat believe that he is so everlastingly superior to all the men that have ever lived, but there's no denying the fact that such is his belief, and he acts according. There was a Professor here one day, lecturing on all sorts of animals, and I asked him if he could explain this aggravating conduct of cats. He said that it was because cats used to be gods, thousands of years ago in the land of Egypt; but I didn't believe him. Egypt is a Scripture country, and consequently we ought not to believe anything about it that we don't read in the Bible. Show me anywhere in the Bible that Egyptian cats are mentioned as having practised as gods, and I'll believe it. Till you show it to me, I'll take the liberty of disbelieving any worldly statement that Professors or anybody else may make about Egypt.

"The most notorious cat I ever met was old Captain Smedley's Yellow Terror. His real legal name was just plain Tom: but being yellow, and being a holy terror in many respects, it got to be the fashion among his acquaintances to call him 'The Yellow Terror'. He was a tremendous big cat, and he had been with Captain Smedley for five years before I saw him.

"Smedley was one of the best men I ever knew. I'll admit that he was a middling hard man on his sailors, so that his ship got the reputation of being a slaughter-house, which it didn't really deserve. And there is no denying that he was a very religious man, which was another thing which made him unpopular with the men. I'm a religious man myself, even when I'm at sea, but I never held with serving out religion to a crew, and making them swallow it with belaying pins. That's what old Smedley used to do.

He was in command of the barque *Medford,* out of Boston, when I knew him. I mean the city of Boston in Massachusetts, and not the little town that folks over in England call Boston: and I must say that I can't see why they should copy the names of our cities, no matter how celebrated they may be. Well! The *Medford* used to sail from Boston to London with grain, where she discharged her cargo and loaded again for China. On the outward passage we used to stop at Madeira, and the Cape, and generally Bangkok, and so on to Canton, where we filled up with tea, and then sailed for home direct.

"Now thishyer Yellow Terror had been on the ship's books for upwards of five years when I first met him. Smedley had him regularly shipped, and signed his name to the ship articles, and held a pen in his paw while he made a cross. . . . You see, in those days the underwriters wouldn't let a ship go to sea without a cat, so as to keep the rats from getting at the cargo. I don't know what a land cat may do, but there ain't a seafaring cat that would look at a rat. What with the steward, and the cook and the men forrard, being always ready to give the ship's cat a bite, the cat is generally full from kelson to deck, and wouldn't take the trouble to speak to a rat, unless one was to bite her tail. But, then, underwriters never know anything about what goes on at sea, and it's a shame that a sailorman should be compelled to give in to their ideas. The Yellow Terror had the general idea that the *Medford* was his private yacht, and that all hands were there to wait on him. And Smedley sort of confirmed him in that idea, by treating him with more respect than he treated his owners, when he was ashore. I don't blame the cat, and after I got to know what sort of a person the cat really was, I can't say as I blamed Smedley to any great extent.

"Tom, which I think I told you was the cat's real name, was far and away the best fighter of all cats in Europe, Asia, Africa, and America. Whenever we sighted land he would get himself up in his best fur, spending hours brushing and polishing it, and biting his claws so as to make sure that they were as sharp as they could be made. As soon as the ship was made fast to the quay, or anchored in the harbour, the Yellow Terror went ashore to look for trouble. He always got it too, though he had such a reputation as a fighter, that whenever he showed himself, every cat that recognised him broke for cover. Why, the gatekeeper at the London Docks—I mean the one at the Shadwell entrance—told me that he always knew when the *Medford* was warping into dock, by the stream of cats that went out of the gate, as if a pack of hounds were after them. You see that as soon as the *Medford* was reported, and word passed among the cats belonging to the ships in dock that the Yellow Terror had arrived, they judged that it was time for them to go ashore, and stop till the *Medford* should sail. Whitechapel used to be regularly overflowed with cats, and the newspapers used to have letters from scientific chaps trying to account for what they called the wave of cats that had spread over East London.

"I remember that once we laid alongside of a Russian brig, down in the basin by Old Gravel Lane. There was a tremendous big black cat sitting on the poop, and as soon as he caught sight of our Tom, he sung out to him, remarking that he was able and ready to wipe the deck up with him at any time. We all understood that the Russian was a new arrival who hadn't ever heard of the Yellow Terror, and we knew that he was, as the good book says, rushing on his fate. Tom was sitting on the rail near the mizzen rigging when the Russian made his remarks, and he didn't seem to hear them. But presently we saw him going slowly aloft till he reached our crossjack yard. He laid out on the yard arm till he was near enough to jump on to the mainyard of the Russian, and the first thing that the Russian cat knew Tom landed square on his back. The fight didn't last more than one round, and at the end of that, the remains of the Russian cat sneaked behind a water cask, and the Yellow Terror came back by the way of the crossjack yard and went on fur brushing, as if nothing had happened.

"When Tom went ashore in a foreign port he generally stopped ashore till we sailed. A few hours before we cast off hawsers, Tom would come aboard. He always knew when we were going to sail, and he never once got left. I remember one time when we were just getting up anchor in Cape Town harbour, and we all reckoned that this time we should have to sail without Tom, he having evidently stopped ashore just a little too long. But presently alongside comes a boat, with Tom lying back at full length in the sternsheets, for all the world like a drunken sailor who has been delaying the ship, and is proud of it. The boatman said that Tom had come down to the pier and jumped into his boat, knowing that the man would row him off to the ship, and calculating that Smedley would be glad to pay the damage. It's my belief that if Tom hadn't found a boatman, he would have chartered the government launch. He had the cheek to do that or anything else.

"Fighting was really Tom's only vice; and it could hardly be called a vice, seeing as he always licked the other cat, and hardly ever came out of a fight with a torn ear or a black eye. Smedley always said that Tom was religious. I used to think that was rubbish; but after I had been with Tom for a couple of voyages I began to believe what Smedley said about him. Every Sunday when the weather permitted, Smedley used to hold service on the quarter-deck. He was a Methodist, and when it came to ladling out Scripture, or singing a hymn, he could give odds to almost any preacher. All hands, except the man at the wheel, and the lookout, were required to attend service on Sunday morning, which naturally caused considerable grumbling, as the watch below considered they had a right to sleep in peace, instead of being dragged aft for service. But they had to knock under, and what they considered even worse, they had to sing, for the old man kept a bright lookout while the singing was going on, and if he caught any man malingering and not doing his full part of the singing he would have a few words to say to that man with a belaying pin, or a rope's end, after the service was over.

"Now Tom never failed to attend service, and to do his level best to help. He would sit somewhere near the old man and pay attention to what was going on better than I've seen some folks do in first-class churches ashore. When the men sang, Tom would start in and let out a yell here and there, which showed that he meant well even if he had never been to a singing-school, and didn't exactly understand singing according to Gunter. First along, I thought that it was all an accident that the cat came to service, and I calculated that his yelling during the singing meant that he didn't like it. But after a while I had to admit that Tom enjoyed the Sunday service as much as the Captain himself, and I agreed with Smedley that the cat was a thoroughgoing Methodist.

"Now after I'd been with Smedley for about six years, he got married all of a sudden. I didn't blame him, for in the first place it wasn't any of my business; and, in the next place, I hold that a ship's captain ought to have a wife, and the underwriters would be a sight wiser if they insisted that all captains should be married, instead of insisting that all ships should carry cats. You see that if a ship's captain has a wife, he is naturally anxious to get back to her, and have his best clothes mended, and his food cooked to suit him. Consequently he wants to make good passages and he don't want to run the risk of drowning himself, or of getting into trouble with his owners, and losing his berth. You'll find, if you look into it, that married captains live longer, and get on better than unmarried men, as it stands to reason that they ought to do.

"But it happened that the woman Smedley married was an Agonyostic, which is a sort of person that doesn't believe in anything, except the multiplication table, and such-like human vanities. She didn't lose any time in getting Smedley round to her way of thinking, and instead of being the religious man he used to be, he chucked the whole thing, and used to argue with me by the hour at a time, to prove that religion was a waste of time, and that he hadn't any soul, and had never been created, but had just descended from a family of seafaring monkeys. It made me sick to hear a respectable sailorman talking such rubbish, but of course, seeing as he was my commanding officer, I had to be careful about contradicting him. I wouldn't ever yield an inch to his arguments, and I told him as respectfully as I could, that he was making the biggest mistake of his life. 'Why, look at the cat,' I used to say, 'he's got sense enough to be religious, and if you was to tell him that he was descended from a monkey, he'd consider himself insulted.' But it wasn't any use. Smedley was full of his new agonyostical theories, and the more I disagreed with him, the more set he was in his way.

"Of course he knocked off holding Sunday morning services; and the men ought to have been delighted, considering how they used to grumble at having to come aft and sing hymns, when they wanted to be below. But there is no accounting for sailors. They were actually disappointed when Sunday came and there wasn't any service. They said that we should have an unlucky voyage, and that the old man, now that he had got a rich wife, didn't consider sailors good enough to come aft on the quarter-deck, and take a hand in singing. Smedley didn't care for their opinion, but he was some considerable worried about the Yellow Terror. Tom missed the Sunday morning service, and he said so as plain as he could. Every Sunday, for three or four weeks, he came on deck, and took his usual seat near the captain, and waited for the service to begin. When he found out that there was no use in waiting for it, he showed that he disapproved of Smedley's conduct in the strongest way. He gave up being intimate with the old man, and once when Smedley tried to pat him, and be friendly, he swore at him, and bit him on the leg—not in an angry way, you understand, but just to show his disapproval of Smedley's irreligious conduct.

"When we got to London, Tom never once went ashore, and he hadn't a single fight. He seemed to have lost all interest in worldly things. He'd sit on the poop in a melancholy sort of way, never minding how his fur looked, and never so much as answering if a strange cat sang out to him. After we left London he kept below most of the time, and finally, about the time that we were crossing the line, he took to his bed, as you might say, and got to be as thin and weak as if he had been living in the forecastle of a lime-juicer. And he was that melancholy that you couldn't get him to take an interest in anything. Smedley got to be so anxious about him that he read up in his medical book to try and find out what was the matter with him; and finally made up his mind that the cat had a first-class disease with a big name something like spinal menagerie. That was some little satisfaction to Smedley, but it didn't benefit the cat any; for nothing that Smedley could do would induce Tom to take medicine. He wouldn't so much as sniff at salts, and when Smedley tried to poultice his neck, he considered himself insulted, and roused up enough to take a piece out of the old man's ear.

"About that time we touched at Funchal, and Smedley sent ashore to lay in another tom-cat, thinking that perhaps a fight would brace Tom up a little. But when the new cat was put down alongside of Tom, and swore at him in the most impudent sort of way, Tom just turned over on his other side, and pretended to go asleep. After that we all felt that the Yellow Terror was done for. Smedley sent the new cat ashore again, and told me that Tom was booked for the other world, and that there wouldn't be any more luck for us on that voyage.

"I went down to see the cat, and though he was thin and weak, I couldn't see any signs of serious disease about him. So I says to Smedley that I didn't believe the cat was sick at all.

"'Then what's the matter with him?' says the old man. 'You saw yourself that he wouldn't fight, and when he's got to that point I consider that he is about done with this world and its joys and sorrows.'

"'His nose is all right,' said I. 'When I felt it just now it was as cool as a teetotaller's.'

"'That does look as if he hadn't any fever to speak of,' says Smedley, 'and the book says that if you've got spinal menagerie you're bound to have a fever.'

"'The trouble with Tom,' says I, 'is mental: that's what it is. He's got something on his mind that is wearing him out.'

"'What can he have on his mind?' says the captain. 'He's got everything to suit him aboard this ship. If he was a millionaire he couldn't be better fixed. He won all his fights while we were in Boston, and hasn't had a fight since, which shows that he can't be low-spirited on account of a licking. No, sir! You'll find that Tom's mind is all right.'

"'Then what gives him such a mournful look out of his eyes?' says I. 'When you spoke to him this morning he looked at you as if he was on the point of crying over your misfortunes—that is to say, if you've got any. Come to think of it, Tom begun to go into thishyer decline just after you were married. Perhaps that's what's the matter with him.'

"But there was no convincing Smedley that Tom's trouble was mental, and he was so sure that the cat was going to die, that he got to be about as low-spirited as Tom himself. 'I begin to wish,' says Smedley to me one morning, 'that I was a Methodist again, and believed in a hereafter. It does seem kind of hard that a first-class cat-fighter like Tom shouldn't have a chance when he dies. He was a good religious cat if ever there was one, and I'd like to think that he was going to a better world.'

"Just then an idea struck me. 'Captain Smedley,' says I, 'you remember how Tom enjoyed the meetings that we used to have aboard here on Sunday mornings!'

"'He did so,' said Smedley. 'I never saw a person who took more pleasure in his Sunday privileges than Tom did.'

"'Captain Smedley,' says I, putting my hand on the old man's sleeve. 'All that's the matter with Tom is seeing you deserting the religion that you was brought up in, and turning agonyostical, or whatever you call it. I call it turning plain infidel. Tom's mourning about your soul, and he's miserable because you don't have any more Sunday morning meetings. I told you the trouble was mental, and now you know it is.'

"'Mebbe you're right,' says Smedley, taking what I'd said in a peaceable way, instead of flying into a rage, as I expected he would. 'To tell you the truth, I ain't so well satisfied in my own mind as I used to be, and I was thinking last night, when I started in to say "Now I lay me"—just from habit you know—that if I'd stuck to the Methodist persuasion I should be a blamed sight happier than I am now.'

"'Tomorrow's Sunday,' says I, 'and if I was you, Captain, I should have the bell rung for service, same as you used to do, and bring Tom up on deck, and let him have the comfort of hearing the rippingest hymns you can lay your hand to. It can't hurt you, and it may do him a heap of good. Anyway, it's worth trying, if you really want the Yellow Terror to get well.'

"'I don't mind saying,' says Smedley, 'that I'd do almost anything to save his life. He's been with me now going on for seven years, and we've never had a hard word. If a Sunday morning meeting will be any comfort to him, he shall have it. Mebbe if it doesn't cure him, it may sort of smooth his hatchway to the tomb.'

"Now the very next day was Sunday, and at six the Captain had the bell rung for service, and the men were told to lay aft. The bell hadn't fairly stopped ringing, when Tom comes up the companion way, one step at a time, looking as if he was on his way to his own funeral. He came up to his usual place alongside of the capstan, and lay down on his side at the old man's feet, and sort of looked up at him with what anybody would have said was a grateful look. I could see that Smedley was feeling pretty serious. He understood what the cat wanted to say, and when he started in to give out a hymn, his voice sort of choked. It was a ripping good hymn, with a regular hurricane chorus, and the men sung it for all they were worth, hoping that it would meet Tom's views. He was too weak to join in with any of his old-time yells, but he sort of flopped the deck with his tail, and you could see he was enjoying it down to the ground.

"Well, the service went on just as it used to do in old times, and Smedley sort of warmed up as it went along, and by and by he'd got the regular old Methodist glow on his face. When it was all through, and the men had gone forrard again, Smedley stooped down, and picked up Tom, and kissed him, and the cat nestled up in the old man's neck and licked his chin. Smedley carried Tom down into the saloon, and sung out to the steward to bring some fresh meat. The cat turned to and ate as good a dinner as he'd ever eaten in his best days, and after he was through, he went into Smedley's own cabin, and curled up in the old man's bunk, and went to sleep purring fit to take the deck off. From that day Tom improved steadily, and by the time we got to Cape Town he was well enough to go ashore, though he was still considerable weak. I went ashore at the same time, and kept an eye on Tom, to see what he would do. I saw him pick out a small measly-looking cat, that couldn't have stood up to a full-grown mouse, and lick him in less than a minute. Then I knew that Tom was all right again, and I admired his judgment in picking out a small cat that was suited to his weak condition. By the time that we got to Canton, Tom was as well in body and mind as he had ever been; and when we sailed, he came aboard with two inches of his tail missing, and his starboard ear carried away, but he had the air of having licked all creation, which I don't doubt he had done, that is to say, so far as all creation could be found in Canton.

"I never heard any more of Smedley's agonyostical nonsense. He went back to the Methodists again, and he always said that Tom had been the blessed means of showing him the error of his ways. I heard that when he got back to Boston, he gave Mrs. Smedley notice that he expected her to go to the Methodist meeting with him every Sunday, and that if she didn't, he should consider that it was a breach of wedding articles, and equivalent to mutiny. I don't know how she took it, or what the consequences were, for I left the *Medford* just then, and took command of a barque that traded between Boston and the West Indies. And I never heard of the Yellow Terror after that voyage, though I often thought of him, and always held that for a cat he was the ablest cat, afloat or ashore, that any man ever met."

Midshipman, the Cat

[JOHN COLEMAN ADAMS]

This is a true story about a real cat who, for aught I know, is still alive and following the sea for a living. I hope to be excused if I use the pronouns "who" and "he" instead of "which" and "it," in speaking of this particular cat; because although I know very well that the grammars all tell us that "he" and "who" apply to persons, while "it" and "which" apply to things, yet this cat of mine always seemed to us who knew him to be so much like a human being that I find it unsatisfactory to speak of him in any other way. There are some animals of whom you prefer to say "he," just as there are persons whom you sometimes feel like calling "it."

The way we met this cat was after this fashion: It was back somewhere in the seventies, and a party of us were cruising east from Boston in the little schooner-yacht *Eyvor*. We had dropped into Marblehead for a day and a night, and some of the boys had gone ashore in the tender. As they landed on the wharf, they found a group of small boys running sticks into a woodpile, evidently on a hunt for something inside.

"What have you in there?" asked one of the yachtsmen.

"Nothin' but a cat," said the boys.

"Well, what are you doing to him?"

"Oh, pokin' him up! When he comes out we'll rock him," was the answer, in good Marblehead dialect.

"Well, don't do it anymore. What's the use of tormenting a poor cat? Why don't you take somebody of your size?"

The boys slowly moved off, a little ashamed and a little afraid of the big yachtsman who spoke; and when they were well out of sight the yachtsmen went on, too, and thought no more about the cat they had befriended. But when they had wandered about the tangled streets of the town for a little while, and paid the visits which all good yachtsmen pay, to the grocery and the post office and the apothecary's soda fountain, they returned to the wharf and found their boat. And behold, there in the stern sheets sat the little gray-and-white cat of the woodpile! He had crawled out of his retreat and made straight for the boat of his champions. He seemed in no wise disturbed or disposed to move when they jumped on board, nor did he show anything but pleasure when they stroked and patted him. But when one of the boys started to put him ashore, the plucky little fellow showed his claws; and no sooner was he set on his feet at the edge of the wharf than he turned about and jumped straight back into the boat.

"He wants to go yachting," said one of the party, whom we called "The Bos'n."

"Ye might as wal take the cat," said a grizzly old fisherman standing on the wharf. "He doesn't belong to anybody, and ef he stays here the boys'll worry him t'death."

"Let's take him aboard," said the yachtsmen. "It's good luck to have a cat on board ship."

Whether it was good luck to the ship or not, it was very clear that pussy saw it meant good luck to him, and curled himself down in the bottom of the boat, with a look that meant business. Evidently he had thought the matter all over and made up his mind that this was the sort of people he wanted to live with; and, being a Marblehead cat, it made no difference to him whether they lived afloat or ashore; he was going where they went, whether they wanted him or not. He had heard the conversation from his place in the woodpile, and had decided to show his gratitude by going to sea with these protectors of his. By casting in his lot with theirs he was paying them the highest compliment of which a cat is capable. It would have been the height of impoliteness not to recognize his distinguished appreciation. So he was allowed to remain in the boat, and was taken off to the yacht.

Upon his arrival there, a council was held, and it was unanimously decided that the cat should be received as a member of the crew; and as we were a company of amateur sailors, sailing our own boat, each man having his particular duties, it was decided that the cat should be appointed midshipman, and should be named after his position. So he was at once and ever after known as "Middy." Everybody took a great interest in him, and he took an impartial interest in everybody—though there were two people on board to whom he made himself particularly agreeable. One was the quiet, kindly professor, the captain of the *Eyvor;* the other was Charlie, our cook and only hired hand. Middy, you see, had a seaman's true instinct as to the official persons with whom it was his interest to stand well.

It was surprising to see how quickly Middy made himself at home. He acted as if he had always been at sea. He was never seasick, no matter how rough it was or how uncomfortable any of the rest of us were. He roamed wherever he wanted to, all over the boat. At mealtimes he came to the table with the rest, sat up on a valise, and lapped his milk and took what bits of food were given him, as if he had eaten that way all his life. When the sails were hoisted it was his especial joke to jump upon the main gaff and be hoisted with it; and once he stayed on his perch till the sail was at the masthead. One of us had to go aloft and bring him down. When we had come to anchor and everything was snug for the night, he would come on deck and scamper out on the main boom, and race from there to the bowsprit end as fast as he could gallop, then climb, monkey-fashion, halfway up the masts, and drop back to the deck or dive down into the cabin and run riot among the berths.

One day, as we were jogging along, under a pleasant southwest wind, and everybody was lounging and dozing after dinner, we heard the Bos'n call out, "Stop that, you fellows!" and a moment after, "I tell you, quit! Or I'll come up and make you!"

We opened our lazy eyes to see what was the matter, and there sat the Bos'n, down in the cabin, close to the companionway, the tassel of his knitted cap coming nearly up to the combings of the hatch; and on the deck outside sat Middy, digging his claws into the tempting yarn, and occasionally going deep enough to scratch the Bos'n's scalp.

When night came and we were all settled down in bed, it was Middy's almost invariable custom to go

the rounds of all the berths, to see if we were prop-
erly tucked in, and to end his inspection by jumping
into the captain's bed, treading himself a comfortable nest there among the blankets, and curling himself down to sleep. It was his own idea to select the
captain's berth as the only proper place in which to
turn in.

But the most interesting trait in Middy's character
did not appear until he had been a week or so on
board. Then he gave us a surprise. It was when we
were lying in Camden Harbor. Everybody was
going ashore to take a tramp among the hills, and
Charlie, the cook, was coming too, to row the boat
back to the yacht.

Middy discovered that he was somehow "getting
left." Being a prompt and very decided cat, it did not
take him long to make up his mind what to do. He
ran to the low rail of the yacht, put his forepaws on
it, and gave us a long, anxious look. Then as the boat
was shoved off he raised his voice in a plaintive mew.
We waved him a good-bye, chaffed him pleasantly,
and told him to mind the anchor, and have dinner
ready when we got back.

That was too much for his temper. As quick as a
flash he had dived overboard, and was swimming
like a water spaniel, after the dinghy!

That was the strangest thing we had ever seen in
all our lives! We were quite used to elephants that

could play at seesaw, and horses that could fire can-
non, to learned pigs and to educated dogs; but a cat
that of his own accord would take to the water like
a full-blooded Newfoundland was a little beyond
anything we had ever heard of. Of course the boat
was stopped, and Middy was taken aboard drenched
and shivering, but perfectly happy to be once more
with the crew. He had been ignored and slighted;
but he had insisted on his rights, and as soon as they
were recognized he was quite contented.

Of course, after that we were quite prepared for
anything that Middy might do. And yet he always
managed to surprise us by his bold and independent
behavior. Perhaps his most brilliant performance was
a visit he paid a few days after his swim in Camden
Harbor.

We were lying becalmed in a lull of the wind off
the entrance to Southwest Harbor. Near us, perhaps
a cable's-length away, lay another small yacht, a
schooner hailing from Lynn. As we drifted along on
the tide, we noticed that Middy was growing very
restless; and presently we found him running along
the rail and looking eagerly toward the other yacht.
What did he see—or smell—over there which interested him? It could not be the dinner, for they were
not then cooking. Did he recognize any of his old
chums from Marblehead? Perhaps there were some
cat friends of his on the other craft. Ah, that was it!

There they were on the deck, playing and frisking together—two kittens! Middy had spied them, and was longing to take a nearer look. He ran up and down the deck, mewing and snuffing the air. He stood up on his favorite position when on lookout, with his forepaws on the rail. Then, before we realized what he was doing, he had plunged overboard again, and was making for the other boat as fast as he could swim! He had attracted the attention of her company, and no sooner did he come up alongside than they prepared to welcome him. A fender was lowered, and when Middy saw it he swam toward it, caught it with his forepaws, clambered along it to the gunwale, and in a twinkling was over the side and on the deck scraping acquaintance with the strange kittens.

How they received him I hardly know, for by that time our boat was alongside to claim the runaway. And we were quite of the mind of the skipper of the *Winnie L.,* who said, as he handed our bold midshipman over the side, "Well, that beats all *my* going a-fishing!"

Only a day or two later Middy was very disobedient when we were washing decks one morning. He trotted about in the wet till his feet were drenched, and then retired to dry them on the white spreads of the berths below. That was quite too much for the captain's patience. Middy was summoned aft, and, after a sound rating, was hustled into the dinghy which was moored astern, and shoved off to the full length of her painter. The punishment was a severe one for Middy, who could bear anything better than exile from his beloved shipmates. So of course he began to exercise his ingenious little brain to see how he could escape. Well under the overhang of the yacht he spied, just about four inches out of water, a little shoulder of the rudder. That was enough for him. He did not stop to think whether he would be any better off there. It was a part of the yacht, and that was home. So overboard he went, swam for the rudder, scrambled on to it, and began howling piteously to be taken on deck again; and, being a spoiled and much-indulged cat, he was soon rescued from his uncomfortable roosting place and restored to favor.

I suppose I shall tax your powers of belief if I tell you many more of Middy's doings. But truly he was a strange cat, and you may as well be patient, for you will not soon hear of his equal. The captain was much given to rifle practice, and used to love to go ashore and shoot at a mark. On one of his trips he allowed Middy to accompany him, for the simple reason, I suppose, that Middy decided to go, and got on board the dinghy when the captain did. Once ashore, the marksman selected a fine large rock as a rest for his rifle, and opened fire upon his target. At the first shot or two Middy seemed a little surprised, but showed no disposition to run away. After the first few rounds, however, he seemed to have made up his mind that since the captain was making all that racket it must be entirely right and proper, and nothing about which a cat need bother his head in the least. So, as if to show how entirely he confided in the captain's judgment and good intentions, that imperturbable cat calmly lay down, curled up, and went to sleep in the shade of the rock over which the captain's rifle was blazing and cracking about once in two minutes. If anybody was ever acquainted with a cooler or more self-possessed cat I should be pleased to hear the particulars.

I wish that this chronicle could be confined to nothing but our shipmate's feats of daring and nerve. But, unfortunately, he was not always blameless in his conduct. When he got hungry he was apt to forget his position as midshipman, and to behave just like any cat with an empty stomach. Or perhaps he may have done just what any hungry midshipman does under the circumstances; I do not quite know what a midshipman does under all circumstances and so I cannot say. But here is one of this cat midshipman's exploits. One afternoon, on our way home, we were working along with a head wind and sea toward Wood Island, a haven for many of the small yachts between Portland and the Shoals.

The wind was light and we were a little late in making port. But as we were all agreed that it would be pleasanter to postpone our dinner till we were at anchor, the cook was told to keep things warm and wait till we were inside the port before he set the table. Now, his main dish that day was to be a fine piece of baked fish; and, unfortunately, it was nearly done when we gave orders to hold back the dinner. So he had closed the drafts of his little stove, left the door of the oven open, and turned into his bunk for a quiet doze—a thing which every good sailor does on all possible occasions; for a seafaring life is very uncertain in the matter of sleep, and one never quite knows when he will lose some, nor how much he will lose. So it is well to lay in a good stock of it whenever you can.

It seems that Middy was on watch, and when he saw Charlie fast asleep he undertook to secure a little early dinner for himself. He evidently reasoned with himself that it was very uncertain when we should have dinner and he'd better get his while he could. He quietly slipped down to the stove, walked coolly up to the oven, and began to help himself to baked haddock.

He must have missed his aim or made some mistake in his management of the business, and, by some lucky chance for the rest of us, waked the cook. For, the first we knew, Middy came flying up the cabin companionway, followed by a volley of shoes and spoons and pieces of coal, while we could hear Charlie, who was rather given to unseemly language when he was excited, using the strongest words in his dictionary about "that thief of a cat!"

"What's the matter?" we all shouted at once.

"Matter enough, sir!" growled Charlie. "That little cat's eaten up half the fish! It's a chance if you get any dinner tonight, sir."

You may be very sure that Middy got a sound wigging for that trick, but I am afraid the captain forgot to deprive him of his rations as he threatened. He was much too kindhearted.

The very next evening Middy startled us again by a most remarkable display of coolness and courage. After a weary thrash to windward all day, under a provokingly light breeze, we found ourselves under the lee of the little promontory at Cape Neddick, where we cast anchor for the night. Our supply of water had run very low, and so, just after sunset, two of the party rowed ashore in the tender to replenish our water keg, and by special permission Middy went with them.

It took some time to find a well, and by the time the jugs were filled it had grown quite dark. In launching the boat for the return to the yacht, by some ill luck a breaker caught her and threw her back upon the beach. There she capsized and spilled out the boys, together with their precious cargo. In the confusion of the moment, and the hurry of setting matters to rights, Middy was entirely forgotten, and when the boat again was launched, nobody thought to look for the cat. This time everything went well, and in a few minutes the yacht was sighted through the dusk. Then somebody happened to think of Middy! He was nowhere to be seen. Neither man remembered anything about him after the capsize. There was consternation in the hearts of those unlucky wights. To lose Middy was almost like losing one of the crew.

But it was too late and too dark to go back and risk another landing on the beach. There was nothing to be done but to leave poor Middy to his fate, or at least to wait until morning before searching for him.

But just as the prow of the boat bumped against the fender on the yacht's quarter, out from under the stern sheets came a wet, bedraggled, shivering cat, who leaped on board the yacht and hurried below into the warm cabin. In that moist adventure in the surf, Middy had taken care of himself, rescued himself from a watery grave, got on board the boat as soon as she was ready, and sheltered himself in the warmest corner. All this he had done without the least outcry, and without asking any help whatever. His self-reliance and courage were extraordinary.

Well, the pleasant month of cruising drew to a close, and it became a question what should be done with Middy. We could not think of turning him adrift in the cold world, although we had no fears but that so bright and plucky a cat would make a living anywhere. But we wanted to watch over his fortunes, and perhaps take him on the next cruise with us when he should have become a more settled and dignified Thomas. Finally, it was decided that he should be boarded for the winter with an artist, Miss Susan H———, a friend of one of our party. She wanted a studio cat, and would be particularly pleased to receive so accomplished and traveled a character as Middy. So when the yacht was moored to the little wharf at Annisquam, where she always ended her cruises, and we were packed and ready for our journey to Boston, Middy was tucked into a basket and taken to the train. He bore the confinement with the same good sense which had marked all his life with us, though I think his feelings were hurt at the lack of confidence we showed in him. And, in truth, we were a little ashamed of it ourselves, and when once we were on the cars somebody suggested that he be released from his prison just to see how he would behave. We might have known he would do himself credit. For when he had looked over his surroundings, peeped above the back of the seat at the passengers, taken a good look at the conductor, and counted the rest of the party to see that none of us was missing, Middy snuggled down upon the seat, laid his head upon the captain's knee, and slept all the way to Boston.

That was the last time I ever saw Middy. He was taken to his new boarding place in Boylston Street, where he lived very pleasantly for a few months, and made many friends by his pleasing manners and unruffled temper. But I suppose he found it a little dull in Boston. He was not quite at home in his aesthetic surroundings. I have always believed he sighed for the freedom of a sailor's life. He loved to sit by the open window when the wind was east, and seemed to be dreaming of faraway scenes. One day he disappeared. No trace of him was ever found. A great many things may have happened to him. But I never could get rid of the feeling that he went down to the wharves and the ships and the sailors, trying to find his old friends, looking everywhere for the stanch little *Eyvor;* and, not finding her, I am convinced that he shipped on some East Indiaman and is now a sailor cat on the high seas.

Peter: A Cat o' One Tail

[**CHARLES MORLEY**]

Peter, the admirable cat whose brief history I am about to relate, appeared in the world on a terrible winter's night. A fierce snowstorm was raging, the sleet was driving at a terrific rate through the air, and the streets were banked up with snow-drifts. All traffic had been stopped, the roar of London was hushed, and every one who had the merest pretence of a fireside sought it on this memorable occasion. It was a wild night in the city, a wild night in the country, a wild night at sea, and certainly a most unpropitious night for the birth of a cat, an animal which is always associated with home and hearth. The fact remains that Peter was born on the night of one of the most terrible storms on record.

Our chairs were drawn up to the fire, the tea-things were on the table, and my mother was just about to try the strength of the brew, when Ann Tibbits, our faithful and well-tried maid-of-all-work, bounced into the room without knocking at the door. Her cap was all awry, her hair was disheveled, and she gasped for breath as she addressed herself to my mother thus, in spasms:

"Please—ma'am—the cat has put her kittens—in—your—bonnet!"

Such a breach of discipline had never been known before in our prim household, where there was a place for everything, and everything had a place.

My mother pushed her spectacles on to her forehead, and, looking severely at Ann, said: "*Which* one, Ann? My summer bonnet, or—my winter bonnet?"

"The one with the fur lining, ma'am."

"And a most comfortable bonnet to live in, I'm sure!" replied my mother sarcastically, as much as to say that she wished all cats had such a choice under the circumstances. "Another cat would have chosen the one with the lace and the violets, out of sheer perverseness. But there—I *knew* I could depend on a cat which had been trained in *my* house."

My mother poured out a cup of tea, betraying no agitation as she dropped two lumps of sugar into the cup—her customary allowance—and helped herself to cream. In a minute or two, however, she took up her knitting, and I noticed that two stitches in succession were dropped, a sure sign that she was perturbed in spirit. Suddenly my mother turned her eyes to the fire.

"*How many,* Ann?" she continued, addressing our faithful servant, who still remained standing at the table awaiting her orders.

"Seven, ma'am."

"*Seven!*" cried my mother. "Seven—it's outrageous. Why, my bonnet wouldn't hold 'em!"

"Three in the bonnet, ma'am, and two in your new m–u–f–f!"

"My new muff!" cried my mother. "I *knew* you were keeping something back." And the stitches dropped fast and furious. "That's only *five,* Ann," she continued, looking up from her work. "Where are the other two? I insist upon knowing."

"In the Alaska tail boa, ma'am," responded Ann, timidly.

Slowly my mother's wrath evaporated, and her features settled down to their ordinary aspect of composure.

"Well," she said, "it might have been worse. She might have put them in my silk dress. But there—it is evident that something must be done. I'm a kind woman, I hope, but I'm not going to be responsible for seven young and tender kittens. Ann Tibbits, England expects every woman to do her duty!"

"*All?*" asked Ann.

"*Four,*" replied my mother.

"Now?" asked Ann.

"The sooner the better," said my mother.

At this moment a sudden blast shook every window in the house, which seemed to be in momentary danger of a total collapse.

"Not fit to turn a dog out," murmured my mother. "Not fit to turn a dog out. Ugh! how cold it is, and here am I condemning to death four poor little kittens on a night like this—to snatch them away from their warm mother, my muff, and Alaska tail, and dip them in a bucket of ice-cold water. And yet they must go; but, Ann, I've an idea—WARM the water. They shall leave the world comfortably. They'll never know it."

The faithful, unemotional Ann carried out her instructions. Peter was one of the three kittens which were born in my mother's fur-lined bonnet, and the white marks on his body always remind me of the terrible snowstorm in the midst of which he sounded his first mew.

After several weeks the liberty which our cat Cordelia had taken with my mother's finery was forgotten, and the household had settled down into its usual humdrum routine. Tibbits had made the new arrivals a bed in the little box-room, and the doctor declared that Mrs. Cordelia was doing as well as could be expected. Every morning we had asked the usual question: "How is Cordelia?" "Quite well, thank you." "And the kittens?" "Also quite well." In due course Ann brought the welcome news that the three kittens had opened their eyes, and the kid glove was at once detached from the knocker of the front door. It was on the morning after they had obtained their blessed sight that I was invited by Tibbits to go downstairs and take my choice. I went down, but I could see nothing of the kittens; there was only Cordelia, with tail twisting, eyes aflame, and whiskers bristling, wheeling round and round a number of straw cases in which champagne had once been packed. Lo! one of the cases began to walk. The movement caught Cordelia's eye, and she knocked it over with her paw. A fluffy, chubby kitten, consisting of a black body with a patch of white on it, was revealed. The little one so captivated my fancy that I put him in my pocket, and without more ado took him upstairs, and publicly announced my determination to claim him as my property.

"What shall we name it?" asked my mother.

"Fiz," said one, alluding to the empty champagne cases,—a suggestion which was at once overruled, as we were a temperate family and little given to sparkling liquids. "Pop" was also voted against, not only as being vulgar, but as going to the other extreme, and leading people to suppose that we were extensively addicted to ginger-ale.

"I think, my dears, as Peter was born on a—" My mother's speech was interrupted by an exultant "Cock-a-doodle-do."

"That horrid fowl again!" exclaimed my mother.

The cock in question was the property of a neighbor, and was a most annoying bird. Even my kitten was disturbed by the defiant note. *"M-e-w?"* said he, in a meek interrogative, as much as to say, "What *is* that dreadful noise?"

"Cock-a-doodle-do," cried the bird again.

"Mew," replied the kitten, this time with a note of anger in his voice. "COCK-A-DOODLE," screamed the bird, evidently in a violent temper. "Mew," said the kitten again, in a tone of remonstrance. The remaining syllable of his war-cry and the kitten's reply were cut short by my mother, who put her fingers to her ears, and said:

"And the cock crowed thrice. My dears, I have it!"

"What, mother?"

"We'll call him PETER," cried the family.

"Peter Gray?"

"Peter Simple?"

"Peter the Great?"

"No," replied my mother, with a humorous twinkle, "Peter the Apostle," pointing to the Family Bible, which was always kept on a little occasional table in a corner of the sitting-room. "And let Peter be a living warning against fibbing, my dears, whether on a small scale or a large one."

A bowl of water was then placed on the table and, having sprinkled a shower upon his devoted back, I as his proprietor, looking at him closely, cried:

"Arise, Peter; obey thy master."

In the middle of my exhortations, however, Cordelia jumped on the table, took little Peter by the scruff of his neck, and carried him back to the nursery.

The day came when I put Peter into the pocket of my overcoat, and took him away to his new home. I had the greatest confidence in him, being a firm believer in the doctrine of heredity. His father I never knew, but his grandfather bore a great reputation for courage, as was indicated on his tombstone, the inscription on which ran as follows:

Here lies LEAR.

Aged about 8 years.

A Tom Cat killed in

single combat with Tom the Templar

whilst defending his

hearth and home.

England expects every cat

to do his duty.

His mother Cordelia was of an affectionate nature, caring little for the chase, indifferent to birds (except sparrows), temperate in the matter of fish, timid of dogs, a kind mother, and had never been known to scratch a child. I believed then that there was every possibility of Peter's inheriting the admirable qualities of his relatives. The world into which he was introduced contained a large assortment of curios which I had bought in many a salesroom, such as bits of old oak, bits of armor, bits of china, bits of tapestry, and innumerable odds and ends which had taken my fancy. Picture, then, Peter drinking his milk from a Crown Derby dish which I had placed in a corner between the toes of a gentleman skeleton whom Time had stained a tobacco brown. The Crown Derby dish and the skeleton were, like the rest of my furniture, "bargains." At this period of his life Peter resembled a series of irregular circles, such as a geometrician might have made in an absent moment: two round eyes, one round head, and one round body. I regarded him much as a young mother would her first baby, for he was my first pet. I watched him lest he should get into danger; I conversed with him in a strange jargon, which I called cats' language; I played with him constantly, and introduced him to a black hole behind the skeleton's left heel, which was supposed to be the home of mice. He kept a close watch on the black hole, and one day, which is never to be

forgotten, he caught his first mouse. It was a very little one, but it clung to Peter's nose and made it bleed.
Regardless of the pain, Peter marched up to me, tail
in air, and laid the half-dead mouse at my feet, with a
look in his eyes which said plainly enough, "Shades
of Caesar! I claim a Triumph, master."

He returned to the black hole again, and mewed
piteously for more. Peter was very green, as you will
understand, but he soon discovered that mewing
kept the mice away, and having taken the lesson to
heart, preserved silence for the future. The mouse-
hunts occupied but a small portion of Peter's time.
He was full of queer pranks, which youth and high
spirits suggested to him. He took a delight in tum-
bling down the stairs; he hid himself in the mouth
of a lion whose head was one of my chief treasures;
he tilted against a dragon candlestick like a young St.
George; he burnt his budding whiskers in an attempt
to discover the source of the flame in the wick of
the candle. He became, too, a great connoisseur of
vases, ornaments, and pictures, sitting before them
and examining them for an hour at a time. He was
also very much given to voyages of discovery, dark
continents having a peculiar fascination for him.
Even the lion's mouth had no terror for him. I once
produced him from the interior of a brand-new top
hat like a conjurer an omelet. Again, we were very
much surprised at breakfast one morning to see

Peter walk out of a rabbit-pie in which he had secreted himself.

I used to let my canary fly about the room, and Peter chased him. The canary flew to an old helmet on a shelf, and thus baffled Peter. The canary seemed to know this, for when Peter was in the room he always flew to the helmet and sang in peace. If he perched elsewhere there was a chase. The linnet's cage I placed on the window-sill in sunny weather, and Peter took great interest in him. He could not see the musician, but he heard the music, and tried every means he knew to discover its source.

At last he peeped through a little hole at the back of the cage, and when he saw the bird he was quite satisfied, and made no attempt to disturb it.

In the matter of eating and drinking Peter was inclined to vegetarianism, being fond of beet-root and cabbage, but he soon took to carnal habits, always liking his food to be divided into three portions, consisting of greens, potatoes, and meat. In addition to such food as we gave him he by no means despised any delicacies he could discover on his own account. For instance he cleaned out a pot of glycerine. Having tilted the lid up, he pulled out the pins from a pincushion, but was saved in time; he was curious about a powder-box, and came mewing downstairs a Peter in white; he did not despise the birds out of a hat; he lost his temper when he saw his rival in the looking-glass, and was beside himself with rage when the glass swung round and he saw only a plain board. His most curious experience was his first glimpse of the moon, which he saw from our bit of back garden. He was rooted to the ground with wonder at the amazing sight, and we called him in vain. The only reply was a melancholy, love-stricken mew which went to my heart.

So Peter rejoiced in the days of his youth, and there was no end to his frolics. But do not think for a moment that his education was neglected, especially in the invaluable matters of manners and deport-ment, both of which are so essential to advancement in life. I taught him to sit at table; to enter a room with grace, and to leave it with dignity. Indeed, I spared no trouble, and Peter became as rigorous as a Chesterfield in the proper observance of all such matters. I can give you no better example of Peter's extensive knowledge of what was right and wrong in the ceremonial side of life than by telling you that when he felt an irrepressible sneeze forming he trot-ted out of the room and sneezed outside. When Peter played, too, he played gently, and did not dis-turb his elders by obtrusive attentions. He never required to be told twice to do a thing. Once was enough for Peter. Then again in the matter of breakages he was as virtuous a kitten as ever lived. I had thirty precious blue china vases on my sideboard, and through this fragile maze Peter always wound in and out without moving a vase. His virtues in this respect were well known to my servants, who never accused Peter of breaking the milk-jug, or the cups and saucers, I can assure you. Like the best of human beings, he had his faults, but upon these it would be impertinent to touch more than lightly.

Peter was partial to Fridays, because Fridays were devoted to cleaning up. If you have ever watched a woman washing the kitchen floor, you will have noticed that she completes one patch before she proceeds with the next, as if she took pride in each patch, regarding it as a picture. It was Peter's delight to sit and watch this domestic operation; and no sooner was the woman's back turned towards a fresh portion of her territory than Peter ran all over the freshly washed patch and impressed it with the seal of his paws, just as an explorer would indicate a great annexation by a series of flags. That was a mere frolic. It was about this time that I discovered Peter's power as a performing cat. I tied a hare's foot to a piece of string and dangled it before Peter's eyes. I hid the hare's foot in strange places. I flung it downstairs. I threw it upstairs. The hare's foot never failed to attract him. We used to roll on the floor together; we played hide-and-seek together. I noticed that he had a habit of lying on his back with his tail out, his head back, and his paws crossed. By degrees I taught him to assume this attitude at the word of command, so that when I said, "Die, Peter!" Peter turned on his back and became rigid until he received permission to live again.

I also taught him to talk in mews at the word of command. I hear some genial critic exclaim that this cannot be true. I decline to argue with any critic that ever lived, and repeat, fearlessly, and in measured terms, that Peter talked to *me*. Of course he would not drop into conversation with the first person who bade him "good-morning," but I assert again that Peter and I held many conversations together by means of the "mew," used with a score of inflections, often delicately shaded, each of which conveyed its meaning to me.

Peter took to reading, too, quite easily, and sat up with eye-glasses on his nose and a paper between his paws. It was, as you may well imagine, a red-letter day with me when Peter said his prayers for the first time; and I was better pleased when he put his little paws up and lifted his eyes up to the ceiling than with any other of his accomplishments, though they were more appreciated by unthinking friends. It was all very well to place a mouse at my feet and thus play to the gallery, but I felt that Peter's thirst for applause might be his ruin.

When the summer came, and the London pavements began to quake with heat, I determined to fly to the country. As delights are doubled when shared with those we care for, I determined to take Peter with me, so I packed him up in a specially constructed traveling saloon of his own, to wit, a flannel-lined basket containing all the necessary comforts for the journey, such as air-holes and feeding-bottles, and off we started in the highest of spirits. Peter found a new world opened to him, and the thousand and one beauties of the country fascinated us both. We were the guests of a burly farmer, who lived in a queer old house, half timber and half brick, with low-ceilinged rooms. The general living-room was the capacious kitchen, which looked mighty picturesque. Oak panels ran half-way up to the ceiling; the pots and pans were ranged neatly in an open cupboard, pleasantly suggestive of good fare and plenty of it. There were flowers in red pots in the windows, and my bedroom was a picture of coolness and cleanliness.

Amid these pleasant surroundings Peter soon made himself very happy, and became a great friend of a cat called Jack, who took him under his charge and showed him the ways of the country. Jack was a favorite on the farm. He was certainly given to roving, and did not always "come home to tea." As a mouser he had few equals in the countryside, and one evening when we were telling stories by the fireside the farmer told me that Jack had dispatched no less than four hundred mice from one hay-rick.

Jack was a disciple of Isaak Walton. He would crouch on a mossy knoll by the edge of the river, and sometimes was successful in capturing a small trout. The farmer was himself a great fisherman. Jack was a study while the preparations were in progress, and, all intent, would follow close at his master's heels. He would crouch among the rushes whilst the tackle was being adjusted, and anxiously scan the water as the fly drifted along the surface. He took a keen delight in the sport, and when a fish was negotiating the bait he always purred loudly in anticipation of the feast in prospect. The trout landed and the line re-cast, he would seize his prey, and with stealthy gait slink off with his prize, leaving the old farmer to discover his loss when he might. Together Jack and Peter roamed over the meadow lands, and the poultry-run was an object of great interest to them. Together they fought the rats, and together they would lie in wait for the thrush and the blackbird,—I am happy to say in vain. The farmer told me that in his youth Jack once took up his residence in the hollow of an old oak, where he lived on the furred and feathered game. At last he returned home. For hours he wandered about his old home, fearful of discovery, now crouching amongst the flower-beds, and now flying in terror at the sound of the hall clock. At last he ventured into the kitchen, entering by the window and creeping to the kitchen hearth, where he dozed off to the music of the cricket, to be welcomed like another Prodigal Son.

Alas! these delights were cut short, for Peter and I were soon compelled to pack up our traps and proceed to the seaside for professional purposes. Peter was not fond of the sea. When I took him out yachting he was compelled to call for the steward; and one day when exploring the rocks at low water, gazing with rapture at his own charming face as it was reflected in the glassy surface of a deep pool, an inquiring young lobster nipped his tail, and the shore rang with piteous calls for help. Peter has never cared for the sea since then, and so deeply was the disaster impressed upon him that I have known him to reject a choice bit of meat which happened to have a few grains of salt on it. It wafted him back to the ocean, the lobster, and the steward. What powers of imagination were Peter's!

As these memoirs cover a period of seven or eight years, and as space is limited, my readers will kindly consent to take a seat on the convenient carpet of the magician, and be wafted gently to the next station on the road without further question. This is a pleasant byway in suburban London, greatly frequented by organ-grinders, traveling bears, German bands, and peripatetic white mice. This road is always associated in my mind with the mysterious disappearance of Peter. We had often laughed at the odd old lady who lived two doors higher up, for the anxiety which she displayed when any of her pets were missing. It was our turn now.

This same old lady was very fond of her cats, and had nine of them at the time I am writing of. Every morning when the weather was warm, she and her cats would come out and unconsciously form a succession of tableaux for our amusement. A rug was spread out under the pear tree in the middle of the tiny lawn, a great basket-chair was placed in the middle of this rug, and, these preparations having been made, the old lady, who was very stout, and always wore a monster poke bonnet and a shapeless black silk dress, came out, followed by her nine cats, and took possession of the basket-chair. A little maid then appeared with a tray, on which were nine little blue china saucers and a jug of milk. The nine little saucers were ranged in a semicircle, and filled with milk, whereupon the old lady cried out, "Who says breakfast, dearies? Who says breakfast—breakfast?" This invitation was immediately responded to by the nine cats. When they had done the old lady cried, "Who says washee, dearies? Washee, washee, washee?" Whereupon the nine cats sat on their haunches and proceeded to make their toilettes. The requirements of cleanliness having been satisfied, and the nine basins having been taken away by the little maid, the old lady shouted out, "Who says play, dearies? Playee, playee, playee?" holding out her arms, and calling out, "Dido Dums, Dido Dums, come here, deary," when a fine Persian cat jumped on to her right shoulder. "Now Diddles Doddles, Diddles Doddles," and another Persian cat jumped on to her left shoulder. "Tootsy Wootsy," she called once more, and a black cat scrambled up to the crown of the poke bonnet. And one by one they were summoned by some endearing diminutive, until the nine cats had taken possession of every possible coign of vantage which was offered by the old lady's capacious person. There they sat, waving their tails to and fro, evidently very pleased by their mistress's little attentions. Mrs. Mee was not very popular in the neighborhood, except with the milkman and the butcher. The cats'-meat-man, indeed, who supplied various families in our road, positively hated her—so I gathered from our servant,—and had been heard to say *sotto voce* in unguarded moments, "Ha! ha! I'll be revenged." It was not unnatural, as the cats were fed on mutton cutlets and fresh milk, and cats' meat was at a discount. About three weeks before Peter disappeared, Mrs. Mee, in the short space of three or four days, had lost no less than five cats by a violent death, and five little graves had been dug, marked by five little tombstones, and the five dead cats had been laid in their last resting-places by the hands of the old lady herself. A funeral is not generally amusing, but I could not restrain a smile when I saw my eccentric old neighbor follow the remains of her dead pets, which were reverently carried on the tea-tray by the little serving-maid, the old lady herself leading the way, ringing a muffled peal with the dinner-bell, the remaining cats bringing up the rear, pondering over the fate of their dead comrades.

It happened that three of these unfortunate victims had been found on my doorstep. I felt very angry with the old lady, who blamed me for the destruction of her pets, adducing the fact that they were found dying on my doorsteps as proof conclusive. One morning I received an anonymous postcard. Although it bore the Charing Cross postmark, I felt sure it came from the old lady. It read as follows:

"The Assyrian came down like a wolf on the fold."

This was the last straw, for I felt that as regards the old lady's cats I had behaved in a sympathetic and neighborly spirit. I remember this post-card because the same afternoon that it came Peter disappeared, and I began to fear that he had yielded to the temptation of a poisoned pig's foot which had been found in my garden stripped of its flesh. This was a delicacy which Peter had never been able to resist, though why he should have preferred it to the choice foods that were daily piled upon his plate I cannot for the life of me say. We searched the neighborhood in vain, and at last I determined to advertise. Accordingly I addressed an advertisement to my favorite paper. It ran as follows:

"COME BACK, PETER. Lost, stolen, strayed, or poisoned, a white and black cat called Peter, who left his friends at—on Monday afternoon last. Round his neck he wore a blue ribbon with the word PETER embroidered upon it in red silk. Before retiring to rest he always says his prayers. Dead or alive, a reward of Two Pounds is offered to any one who will restore him to his mourning friends."

I little knew what I was bringing on my devoted head. I had been troubled enough before with dying cats, but now they were all alive. Cats were brought to me in baskets, in boxes, in arms; Manx cats and cats whose tails were missing for other than hereditary reasons; lame cats, blind cats, cats with one eye, and cats who squinted. Never before had I seen such an extraordinary collection. My whole time was now taken up in interviewing callers with cats.

If the boys were bad before, they were a thousand times worse now. Here is one example out of a score. He was a boy known as Pop, who carried the laundry baskets.

"'Ave yer found yer cat yet?"

"No, we haven't."

"Did yer say it was a yaller 'un?"

"No, I didn't."

"What did I say, Hop?" continued Pop, triumphantly turning to a one-legged friend who swept a crossing close by.

"Yer said, Pop, as it was a tortus," murmured the bashful Hop, who had sheltered himself behind Pop.

"A tortus, that's it. A tortus, and Hop and *I's* found it, sir. We've got it here."

"You're wrong. My cat's *not* a tortoise," I replied.

"Bless you, we know that, guv'nor. Just as if we didn't know Peter! Ah! Peter was a cat as wants a lot of replacin', Peter does. But me and Hop's got a tortus as is a wunner, guv'nor. A heap better nor Peter. Poor old Peter! he's dead and gone. Be sure of that. This 'ere's a reg'lar bad road. A prize-winner, warn't 'e, Hoppy?" They held up the prize-winner, who *was* not a tortoise, and was mangy.

"Look here, my boys, you can take her away. Now, be off. Quick march!"

"Yer don't want it, guv'nor. Jest think agin. Why, 'ow will you get along without a cat? The mice is 'orrible in this 'ere road. Come, guv'nor, I'll tell you what I'll do. You shall 'ave a bargain," said Pop.

I insisted that the tortoise prize-winner should be taken away, and the next day I stopped the advertisement and resigned myself to despair. A week after Peter had disappeared I heard the voice of my friend Pop at the door. "I say, mister, I've some noose. Come along o' me. I think I've found 'im. Real. A blue ribbon round 'is neck and says 'is prayers. Put on yer 'at and foller, foller, foller me." Mr. Pop led the way along the road, and turned off to the right, and we walked up another road until we reached a large house which had been unoccupied for many months. The drains were up, and two or three workmen were busy. Pop at once introduced me as "the gent as was lookin' for his cat." "Have you seen a cat with a blue ribbon round his neck?" I asked them, very dubious as to the honesty of Pop's intention. "Well, sich a cat *as* bin 'ere for some days," replied the workman to whom I had spoken. "He used to come when we were gettin' our bit of dinner. But we never know'd but wot it came from next door. You go upstairs to the first-floor front, and you'll see a sight." On the top of the stairs was Peter, who knew me at once, and began to purr and rub himself against my legs in a most affectionate manner, as if to appease any outburst of wrath on my part. I felt too pleased to be angry, and followed Peter into the empty room, which was littered with paper and rubbish, and the remains of forty or fifty mice lay strewn about the floor. Peter looked up to me as if to say: "Not a bad bag—eh, master?" In the corner of the room was a bit of sacking which Peter had used as a bed. Pop explained to me that he had heard the men talking about the funny cat that came and dined with them every day. This conversation induced him to search the house, with the happy result that Peter was restored to the bosom of his sorrowing family, and Pop gave up the laundry basket, and invested the reward in a small private business of his own.

Peter and I have had many homes in London and in the country. Together we have lived in flats, in hotels, in farm-houses, and in lodgings for single gentlemen. In lodgings for single gentlemen we had many strange experiences which would occupy too much time to relate, and I will therefore touch but lightly upon this period of Peter's career. Peter, being a gentlemanly cat, never quarreled with ladies, however hard they might be to please, and let them gird at him as they would. For did not that gracious animal, when Mrs. Nagsby was accusing him of stealing fowls, say—did he not arch his bonny back and purr against Mrs. Nagsby's ankles and endeavor to appease her? In her softer moods she did sometimes relax, and even allowed Peter to sit by her side as she read the paper. Peter was held responsible for every article that was lost in Mrs. Nagsby's apartments, and the amount of money I paid to that good lady for break-age in the course of six months would have fur-nished a small cottage. Mrs. Nagsby was a widow, and the late lamented Nagsby had supported her by his performances on the euphonium. This instrument was kept in a case in Mrs. Nagsby's little room, which was on the ground-floor back, and looked on to a series of dingy walls. Mrs. Nagsby used to polish up the euphonium every Saturday morning with a reg-ularity which nothing prevented. Did it not speak volumes for her affection for the late lamented? On one of these Saturdays it happened that a German band stopped at the front door. Mrs. Nagsby could never resist the seductive power of brass music. She rushed upstairs to the first-floor front to listen to the performance. Fate ordained it that Mrs. Nagsby should leave the precious euphonium on the floor in her haste to hear the band. Fate ordained it also that Peter should come down stairs at this particular moment and wend his way to Mrs. Nagsby's parlor. Fate also had ordained it that a mouse which lived in a hole behind Mrs. Nagsby's easy-chair should issue at this particular moment for a little bread-crumb expedition. Mrs. Nagsby was a careful housekeeper, and finding no crumbs about, the mouse roamed into the silent highway presented by the orifice of the euphonium. It was natural enough that Peter should follow the mouse. Unfortunately, Peter's progress was stopped, the girth of his body being too great to admit him; and my door being open, I at once rushed to the rescue, and found Peter with his head in the depths of the euphonium, and making fierce struggles to vacate the position. Mrs. Nagsby came downstairs and entered her parlor just as I succeeded in extracting Peter from the musical instrument. Fiercely was I reproached for Peter's escapade, and humbly did I make his apologies, little knowing the secret of the plight from which I had rescued him. Having soothed my landlady, she at length took up the euphonium and proceeded to apply her eye to the main orifice to see if Peter had damaged it, handling the euphonium in the manner of a telescope. I was thinking of the reproaches in prospect, when I was startled by a loud shriek, to which the euphonium imparted a metallic vibration, and Mrs. Nagsby dropped the instrument on to the floor, the good lady herself following it with a thud. A wee mouse scuttled across her face, disappeared behind the easy chair, and doubtless rejoined his anxious family. Mrs. Nagsby recovered after her maid-of-all-work and I had burnt a few sheets of brown paper under her nostrils; but I had great difficulty in making the peace.

In vain I pointed out that the responsibility did not remain with me, or even with Peter. We agreed after some debate that it was the German band, which was never afterwards patronized by Mrs. Nagsby.

I got into further trouble with Mrs. Nagsby owing to a greyhound which I had bought at a sale. I had no character with him, for he had no character. If Mrs. Nagsby had killed him with the meat hatchet I would have held my peace, for never a day passed but King Arthur took his name in vain. The first night I brought him home Mrs. Nagsby gave me permission as a great favor to chain him to the kitchen table. In the morning two of the table legs had been mangled, and that is our reason why I called him King Arthur, of the Round Table. The next night King Arthur was taken upstairs and attached to the leg of my wash-stand. I was awakened out of my beauty sleep by a horrible clamor which caused me to think that the house had fallen in. I presently realized that King Arthur had mistaken the water-jug for a dragon. In any case it was smashed to bits, and the noise brought Mrs. Nagsby to my door in anger. I should be sorry to say what King Arthur cost me in hard cash for breakages and legs of mutton. Poor Peter! thou wast a saint when compared with that fiend on four legs.

The *denouement* came at last, and it arose from King Arthur's fondness for the ladies. There was nothing remarkable in the appearance of the old lady who was Mrs. Nagsby's favorite lodger, who had held the rooms above mine for three years. But the lady had a most beautiful sealskin jacket, trimmed with tails of sable. King Arthur had unluckily a feminine affection for furs, and I never dared to take him into any of the fashionable thoroughfares, as he had a way of following the ladies, not for their own dear sakes, but for the fur which they might happen to be wearing. Whether they were only tippets or dyed rabbit-skins, it did not matter to King Arthur.

Well, one unfortunate afternoon, I was leading my greyhound home. A few yards in front of us was Mrs. Nagsby's first-floor lady, taking the sun in all the glories of her sealskin jacket and sable tails. To my horror I dropped the chain in taking a match-box out of my pocket, and before I could take any steps to prevent him—*King Arthur was coursing Mrs. Nagsby's first-floor lodger at his highest rate of speed!!!* King Arthur held on his course and literally took the old lady aback, and began to tear those choice sable tippets asunder. Nor was the base creature content to rest at the sable tippets. Before I reached his victim his mouth was full of sealskin. Let me pass on, merely saying that King Arthur was shot that night in the mews at the back of Mrs. Nagsby's, a victim to his own indiscretions.

And now I come to the fatal catastrophe which finally drove me and Peter from the shelter of Mrs. Nagsby's roof. That lady had a set of false teeth which she was in the habit of depositing on her dressing-table when she went to bed. I had learned

this from Sarah when that damsel was in a confiden-
tial mood. Peter, I think I have told you, slept in my
room. One very warm night Mrs. Nagsby left her
door open, and her night light was burning as usual. I
also slept with my door open, and Peter, being hot
like the rest of us, left the room for a stroll, and visited
Mrs. Nagsby's apartment. Presently he came back
with Mrs. Nagsby's teeth between his own—at least I
suppose so, for I found them on the hearth-rug when
I awoke. I was greatly amused, though a little puzzled
to know how I could replace them. After some
reflection I went down to breakfast, placed the trophy
in a saucer, and showed it to Sarah, who screamed
and traitorously ran up and informed her mistress.
Mrs. Nagsby came down rampant, but of course
speechless. I was thankful for this; but the violent
woman, after sputtering spasmodically, caught sight
of the missing article in the saucer, and, lost to all
sense of shame, replaced it in position and poured
forth a torrent of the most violent abuse.

Peter and I left.

My Cat

[MICHEL DE MONTAIGNE]

When my cat and I entertain each other with mutual antics, as playing with a garter, who knows but that I make more sport for her than she makes for me? Shall I conclude her to be simple that has her time to begin or to refuse to play, as freely as I have mine. Nay, who knows but that it a defect of not my understanding her language (for doubtless cats can talk and reason with one another) that we agree no better; and who knows but that she pities me for being no wiser than to play with her; and laughs, and censures my folly in making sport for her, when we two play together.

Calvin: A Study of Character

[CHARLES DUDLEY WARNER]

Calvin is dead. His life, long to him, but short for the rest of us, was not marked by startling adventures, but his character was so uncommon and his qualities were so worthy of imitation, that I have been asked by those who personally knew him to set down my recollections of his career.

His origin and ancestry were shrouded in mystery; even his age was a matter of pure conjecture. Although he was of the Maltese race, I have reason to suppose that he was American by birth as he certainly was in sympathy. Calvin was given to me eight years ago by Mrs. Stowe, but she knew nothing of his age or origin. He walked into her house one day out of the great unknown and became at once at home, as if he had been always a friend of the family. He appeared to have artistic and literary tastes, and it was as if he had inquired at the door, if that was the residence of the author of "Uncle Tom's Cabin," and, upon being assured that it was, had decided to dwell there. This is, of course, fanciful, for his antecedents were wholly unknown, but in his time he could hardly have been in any household where he would not have heard "Uncle Tom's Cabin" talked about. When he came to Mrs. Stowe, he was as large as he ever was, and apparently as old as he ever became. Yet there was in him no appearance of age; he was in the happy maturity of all his powers, and you would rather have said that in that maturity he had found the secret of perpetual youth. And it was as difficult to believe that he would ever be aged as it was to imagine that he had ever been in immature youth. There was in him a mysterious perpetuity.

After some years, when Mrs. Stowe made her winter home in Florida, Calvin came to live with us. From the first moment, he fell into the ways of the house and assumed a recognized position in the family,—I say recognized, because after he became known he was always inquired for by visitors, and in the letters to the other members of the family he always received a message. Although the least obtrusive of beings, his individuality always made itself felt.

His personal appearance had much to do with this, for he was of royal mold, and had an air of high breeding. He was large, but he had nothing of the fat grossness of the celebrated Angora family; though powerful, he was exquisitely proportioned, and as graceful in every movement as a young leopard. When he stood up to open a door—he opened all the doors with old-fashioned latches—he was portentously tall, and when stretched on the rug before the fire he seemed too long for this world—as indeed he was. His coat was the finest and softest I have ever seen, a shade of quiet Maltese; and from his throat downward, underneath, to the white tips of his feet, he wore the whitest and most delicate ermine; and no person was ever more fastidiously neat. In his finely formed head you saw something of his aristocratic character; the ears were small and cleanly cut, there was a tinge of pink in the nostrils, his face was handsome and the expression of his countenance exceedingly intelligent—I should call it even a sweet expression if the term were not inconsistent with his look of alertness and sagacity.

It is difficult to convey a just idea of his gayety in connection with his dignity and gravity, which his name expressed. As we know nothing of his family, of course it will be understood that Calvin was his Christian name. He had times of relaxation into utter playfulness, delighting in a ball of yarn, catching sportively at stray ribbons when his mistress was at her toilet, and pursuing his own tail, with hilarity, for lack of anything better. He could amuse himself by the hour, and he did not care for children; perhaps something in his past was present to his memory. He had absolutely no bad habits, and his disposition was perfect. I never saw him exactly angry, though I have seen his tail grow to an enormous size when a strange cat appeared upon his lawn. He disliked cats, evidently regarding them as feline and treacherous, and he had no association with them. Occasionally there would be heard a night concert in the shrubbery. Calvin would ask to have the door opened, and then you would hear a rush and a "pestzt," and the concert would explode, and Calvin would quietly come in and resume his seat on the hearth. There was no trace of anger in his manner, but he wouldn't have any of that about the house. He had the rare virtue of magnanimity. Although he had fixed notions about his own rights, and extraordinary persistency in getting them, he never showed temper at a repulse; he simply and firmly persisted till he had what he wanted. His diet was one point; his idea was that of the scholars about dictionaries,—to "get the best." He knew as well as any one what was in the house, and would refuse beef if turkey was to be had; and if there were oysters, he would wait over the turkey to see if the oysters would not be forthcoming. And yet he was not a gross gourmand; he would eat bread if he saw me eating it, and thought he was not being imposed on. His habits of feeding, also, were refined; he never used a knife, and he would put up his hand and draw the fork down to his mouth as gracefully as a grown person. Unless necessity compelled, he would not eat in the kitchen, but insisted upon his meals in the dining-room, and would wait patiently, unless a stranger were present; and then he was sure to importune the visitor, hoping that the latter was ignorant of the rule of the house, and would give him something. They used to say that he preferred as his table-cloth on the floor a certain well-known church journal; but this was said by an Episcopalian. So far as I know, he had no religious prejudices, except that he did not like the association with Romanists. He tolerated the servants, because they belonged to the house, and would sometimes linger by the kitchen stove; but the moment visitors came in he arose, opened the door, and marched into the drawing-room. Yet he enjoyed the company of his equals, and never withdrew, no matter how many callers—whom he recognized as of his society,—might come into the drawing-room. Calvin was fond of company, but he wanted to choose it; and I have no doubt that his was an aristocratic fastidiousness, rather than one of faith. It is so with most people.

The intelligence of Calvin was something phenomenal, in his rank of life. He established a method of communicating his wants, and even some of his sentiments; and he could help himself in many things. There was a furnace register in a retired room, where he used to go when he wished to be alone, that he always opened when he desired more heat; but never shut it, any more than he shut the door after himself. He could do almost everything but speak; and you would declare sometimes that you could see a pathetic longing to do that in his intelligent face. I have no desire to overdraw his qualities, but if there was one thing in him more noticeable than another, it was his fondness for nature. He could content himself for hours at a low window, looking into the ravine and at the great trees, noting the smallest stir there; he delighted, above all things, to accompany me walking about the garden, hearing the birds, getting the smell of the fresh earth, and rejoicing in the sunshine. He followed me and gamboled like a dog, rolling over on the turf and exhibiting his delight in a hundred ways. If I worked, he sat and watched me, or looked off over the bank, and kept his ear open to the twitter in the cherry-trees. When it stormed, he was sure to sit at the window, keenly watching the rain or the snow, glancing up and down at its falling; and a winter tempest always delighted him. I think he was genuinely fond of birds, but, so far as I know, he usually confined himself to one a day; he never killed, as some sportsmen do, for the sake of killing, but only as civilized people do,—from necessity. He was intimate with the flying-squirrels who dwell in the chestnut-trees,—too intimate, for almost every day in the summer he would bring in one, until he nearly discouraged them. He was, indeed, a superb hunter, and would have been a devastating one, if his bump of destructiveness had not been offset by a bump of moderation. There was very little of the brutality of the lower animals about him; I don't think he enjoyed rats for themselves, but he knew his business, and for the first few months of his residence with us he waged an awful campaign against the horde, and after that his simple presence was sufficient to deter them from coming on the premises. Mice amused him, but he usually considered them too small game to be taken seriously; I have seen him play for an hour with a mouse, and then let him go with a royal condescension. In this whole matter of "getting a living," Calvin was a great contrast to the rapacity of the age in which he lived.

I hesitate a little to speak of his capacity for friendship and the affectionateness of his nature, for I know from his own reserve that he would not care to have it much talked about. We understood each other perfectly, but we never made any fuss about it; when I spoke his name and snapped my fingers, he came to me; when I returned home at night, he was pretty sure to be waiting for me near the gate, and would rise and saunter along the walk, as if his being there were purely accidental,—so shy was he commonly of showing feeling; and when I opened the door he never rushed in, like a cat, but loitered, and lounged, as if he had had no intention of going in, but would condescend to. And yet, the fact was, he knew dinner was ready, and he was bound to be there. He kept the run of dinner-time. It happened sometimes, during our absence in the summer, that dinner would be early, and Calvin, walking about the grounds, missed it and came in late. But he never made a mistake the second day. There was one thing he never did,—he never rushed through an open door-way. He never forgot his dignity. If he had asked to have the door opened, and was eager to go out, he always went deliberately; I can see him now, standing on the sill, looking about at the sky as if he was thinking whether it were worth while to take an umbrella, until he was near having his tail shut in.

His friendship was rather constant than demonstrative. When we returned from an absence of nearly two years, Calvin welcomed us with evident pleasure, but showed his satisfaction rather by tranquil happiness than by fuming about. He had the faculty of making us glad to get home. It was his constancy that was so attractive. He liked companionship, but he wouldn't be petted, or fussed over, or sit in any one's lap a moment; he always extricated himself from such familiarity with dignity and with no show of temper.

If there was any petting to be done, however, he chose to do it. Often he would sit looking at me, and then, moved by a delicate affection, come and pull at my coat and sleeve until he could touch my face with his nose, and then go away contented. He had a habit of coming to my study in the morning, sitting quietly by my side or on the table for hours, watching the pen run over the paper, occasionally swinging his tail round for a blotter, and then going to sleep among the papers by the inkstand. Or, more rarely, he would watch the writing from a perch on my shoulder. Writing always interested him, and, until he understood it, he wanted to hold the pen.

He always held himself in a kind of reserve with his friend, as if he had said, "Let us respect our personality, and not make a 'mess' of friendship." He saw, with Emerson, the risk of degrading it to trivial conveniency. "Why insist on rash personal relations with your friend?" "Leave this touching and clawing." Yet I would not give an unfair notion of his aloofness, his fine sense of the sacredness of the me and the not-me. And, at the risk of not being believed, I will relate an incident, which was often repeated. Calvin had the practice of passing a portion of the night in the contemplation of its beauties, and would come into our chamber over the roof of the conservatory through the open window, summer and winter, and go to sleep on the foot of my bed. He would do this always exactly in this way; he never was content to stay in the chamber if we compelled him to go upstairs and through the door. He had the obstinacy of General Grant. But this is by the way. In the morning, he performed his toilet and went down to breakfast with the rest of the family. Now, when the mistress was absent from home, and at no other time, Calvin would come in the morning, when the bell rang, to the head of the bed, put up his feet and look into my face, follow me about when I rose, "assist" at the dressing, and in many purring ways show his fondness, as if he had plainly said, "I know that she has gone away, but I am here." Such was Calvin in rare moments.

He had his limitations. Whatever passion he had for nature, he had no conception of art. There was sent to him once a fine and very expressive cat's head in bronze, by Frémiet. I placed it on the floor. He regarded it intently, approached it cautiously and crouchingly, touched it with his nose, perceived the fraud, turned away abruptly, and never would notice it afterward. On the whole, his life was not only a successful one, but a happy one. He never had but one fear, so far as I know: he had a mortal and a reasonable terror of plumbers. He would never stay in the house when they were here. No coaxing could quiet him. Of course he didn't share our fear about their charges, but he must have had some dreadful experience with them in that portion of his life which is unknown to us. A plumber was to him the devil, and I have no doubt that, in his scheme, plumbers were foreordained to do him mischief.

In speaking of his worth, it has never occurred to me to estimate Calvin by the worldly standard. I know that it is customary now, when any one dies, to ask how much he was worth, and that no obituary in the newspapers is considered complete without such an estimate. The plumbers in our house were one day overheard to say that, "They say that *she* says that *he* says that he wouldn't take a hundred dollars for him." It is unnecessary to say that I never made such a remark, and that, so far as Calvin was concerned, there was no purchase in money.

As I look back upon it, Calvin's life seems to me a fortunate one, for it was natural and unforced. He ate when he was hungry, slept when he was sleepy, and enjoyed existence to the very tips of his toes and the end of his expressive and slow-moving tail. He delighted to roam about the garden, and stroll among the trees, and to lie on the green grass and luxuriate in all the sweet influences of summer. You could never accuse him of idleness, and yet he knew the secret of repose. The poet who wrote so prettily of him that his little life was rounded with a sleep, understated his felicity; it was rounded with a good many. His conscience never seemed to interfere with his slumbers. In fact, he had good habits and a contented mind. I can see him now walk in at the study door, sit down by my chair, bring his tail artistically about his feet, and look up at me with unspeakable happiness in his handsome face. I often thought that he felt the dumb limitation which denied him the power of language. But since he was denied speech, he scorned the inarticulate mouthings of the lower animals. The vulgar mewing and yowling of the cat species was beneath him; he sometimes uttered a sort of articulate and well-bred ejaculation, when he wished to call attention to something that he considered remarkable, or to some want of his, but he never went whining about. He would sit for hours at a closed window, when he desired to enter, without a murmur, and when it was opened he never admitted that he had been impatient by "bolting" in. Though speech he had not, and the unpleasant kind of utterance given to his race he would not use, he had a mighty power of purr to express his measureless content with congenial society. There was in him a musical organ with stops of varied power and expression, upon which I have no doubt he could have performed Sebastian Bach's celebrated cat's-fugue.

Whether Calvin died of old age, or was carried off by one of the diseases incident to youth, it is impossible to say; for his departure was as quiet as his advent was mysterious. I only know that he appeared to us in this world in his perfect stature and beauty, and that after a time, like Lohengrin, he withdrew. In his illness, there was nothing more to be regretted than in all his blameless life. I suppose there never was an illness that had more of dignity, and sweetness, and resignation in it. It came on gradually, in a kind of listlessness and want of appetite. An alarming symptom was his preference for the warmth of a furnace-register to the lively sparkle of the open wood-fire. Whatever pain he suffered, he bore it in silence, and seemed only anxious not to obtrude his malady. We tempted him with the delicacies of the season, but it soon became impossible for him to eat, and for two weeks he ate or drank scarcely anything. Sometimes he made an effort to take something, but it was evident that he made the effort to please us. The neighbors—and I am convinced that the advice of neighbors is never good for anything—suggested catnip. He wouldn't even smell it. We had the attendance of an amateur practitioner of medicine, whose real office was the cure of souls, but nothing touched his case. He took what was offered, but it was with the air of one to whom the time for pellets was passed. He sat or lay day after day almost motionless, never once making a display of those vulgar convulsions or contortions of pain which are so disagreeable to society. His favorite place was on the brightest spot of a Smyrna rug by the conservatory, where the sunlight fell and he could hear the fountain play. If we went to him and exhibited our interest in his condition, he always purred in recognition of our sympathy. And when I spoke his name, he looked up with an expression that said, "I understand it, old fellow, but it's no use." He was to all who came to visit him a model of calmness and patience in affliction.

I was absent from home at the last, but heard by daily postal-card of his failing condition; and never again saw him alive. One sunny morning, he rose from his rug, went into the conservatory (he was very thin then), walked around it deliberately, looking at all the plants he knew, and then went to the bay window in the dining-room, and stood a long time looking out upon the little field, now brown and sere, and toward the garden, where perhaps the happiest hours of his life had been spent. It was a last look. He turned and walked away, laid himself down upon the bright spot in the rug, and quietly died.

It is not too much to say that a little shock went through the neighborhood when it was known that Calvin was dead, so marked was his individuality; and his friends, one after another, came in to see him. There was no sentimental nonsense about his obsequies; it was felt that any parade would have been distasteful to him. John, who acted as undertaker, prepared a candle-box for him, and I believe assumed a professional decorum; but there may have been the usual levity underneath, for I heard that he remarked in the kitchen that it was the "dryest wake he ever attended." Everybody, however, felt a fondness for Calvin, and regarded him with a certain respect. Between him and Bertha there existed a great friendship, and she apprehended his nature; she used to say that sometimes she was afraid of him, he looked at her so intelligently; she was never certain that he was what he appeared to be.

When I returned, they had laid Calvin on a table in an upper chamber by an open window. It was February. He reposed in a candle-box, lined about the edge with evergreen, and at his head stood a little wine-glass with flowers. He lay with his head tucked down in his arms,—a favorite position of his before the fire,—as if asleep in the comfort of his soft and exquisite fur. It was the involuntary exclamation of those who saw him, "How natural he looks!" As for myself, I said nothing. John buried him under the twin hawthorn-trees,—one white and the other pink,—in a spot where Calvin was fond of lying and listening to the hum of summer insects and the twitter of birds.

Perhaps I have failed to make appear the individuality of character that was so evident to those who knew him. At any rate, I have set down nothing concerning him but the literal truth. He was always a mystery. I did not know whence he came; I do not know whither he has gone. I would not weave one spray of falsehood in the wreath I lay upon his grave.

Acknowledgments

I gratefully acknowledge all the remarkable cats that have graced my life. First my own Emily and Muffin and my sister's Mandu, Maya, Oca, Cairo, Ina, Amanda, Bonne Nuit, Fromage, and Emile. Also Dudley, who has proved to my father that cats are worthy friends, and Becky's Maggie, Mollie, Mittens, Muffin, Monty, and Mischief. Special mention to Nancy's Aja, Puck, Bailey, Monster, Miklos, and Tiffany, and to Marc's Figaro, the second-fattest cat in Tokyo, and his sisters, Charlotte, Mita, and Tamachi. And finally, Beans, Eckie, Raisin, Clark Cat, Tara, Zapata, Leo, Tucker, William, Princess, Salem, Sabrina, Meesha, Katrina, Mocha, Tucker, Casey, Pearl (Drayton House), Sam, Melon Hat Cat, Mittens, Jasmine, Jezebel, Delilah, Mookie, Judy, Spatula, Nanny Goat, Roscoe,

ACKNOWLEDGMENTS

Licorice, Swee'pea, Pussywillow, Midnight, Angel, Tommy, Putt Putt, Kiwi, and "The Onion."

Special thanks go to Dr. Jason Fusco, Dr. Philip Bergman, Dr. Joanne McKnight, Dr. John Farrelly, Shawn Takada, and all the staff of Manhattan's Animal Medical Center for performing miracles.

And to all cats (past, present, and future) that Lisa, Lulu, Kathy, Jackie, and Martie have in their lives.

Sources

"The Cat" by Andrew Barton Paterson from *Three Elephant Power and Other Stories*, 1917.

"The Achievement of the Cat" by Saki (H. H. Munro) from *The Square Egg and Other Stories*, 1922.

"How Diana Made the Stars and the Rain" by Charles G. Leland from *Aradia: The Gospel of Witches*, 1880.

"The Home Life of a Holy Cat" by Arthur Weigall, circa 1920.

"The Watchers" by Bram Stoker from *The Jewel of the Seven Stars*, 1902.

"The Cats of Ulthar" by H. P. Lovecraft from *The Tryout*, November 1920.

"The Empty Sleeve" by Algernon Blackwood from the *London Magazine*, January 1911.

"The Cat of the Cane-Brake" by Frederick Stuart Greene from *Metropolitan Magazine*, August 1916.

"The Brazilian Cat" by Arthur Conan Doyle from *The Strand*, December 1898.

"The White Cat" by W. W. Jacobs from *Captains All and Others*, 1905.

"Who Was to Blame?" by Anton Chekhov, 1886.

"The Philanthropist and the Happy Cat" by Saki (H. H. Munro) from *Beasts and Super-Beasts*, 1914.

"Plato: The Story of a Cat" by A. S. Downs from *The Junior Classics*, Volume 8, edited by William Patten, 1912.

"A Talk with Mark Twain's Cat" from the *New York Times*, 1905.

"Ye Marvellous Legend of Tom Connor's Cat" by Samuel Lover from *Handy Andy: A Tale of Irish Life*, 1842.

"The Cat and the King" by Ambrose Bierce from *Fantastic Fables*, 1899.

"The Master Cat, or, Puss in Boots" by Charles Perrault from *The Blue Fairy Book*, 1889.

"The Cat Who Played Robinson Crusoe" by Charles G. D. Roberts from the *Ladies Home Journal*, December 1910.

"The Yellow Terror" by W. L. Alden, circa 1900.

"Midshipman, the Cat" by John Coleman Adams, circa 1890.

"Peter: A Cat o' One Tail" by Charles Morley from *The Junior Classics*, Volume 8, edited by William Patten, 1912.

"My Cat" by Michel de Montaigne from *Essays*, 1588.

"Calvin: A Study of a Character" by Charles Dudley Warner from *Scribner's Monthly*, June 1877.